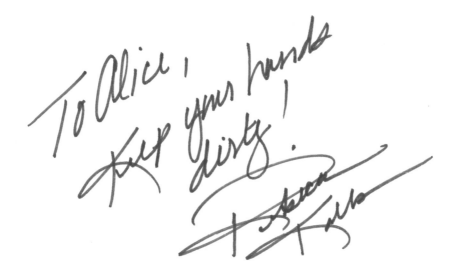

To Alice,
Keep your hands
dirty!

Rebecca's Garden

Rebecca's Garden

Four Seasons
To Grow On

Rebecca Kolls

Illustrated by Roberta S. Rosenthal

AVON BOOKS ◆ NEW YORK

AVON BOOKS
A division of
The Hearst Corporation
1350 Avenue of the Americas
New York, New York 10019

All photographs in the insert are courtesy of the author
unless otherwise specified.

Library of Congress Cataloging in Publication Data:
Kolls, Rebecca.
Rebecca's garden : four seasons to grow on / Rebecca Kolls ;
illustrated by Roberta S. Rosenthal. — 1st ed.
p.   cm.
Includes index.
1. Gardening.   I. Title.
SB453.K687 1998   97-46732
635—dc21   CIP

First Avon Books Printing: May 1998

AVON TRADEMARK REG. U.S. PAT. OFF. AND IN OTHER COUNTRIES, MARCA REGISTRADA,
HECHO EN U.S.A.

Printed in the U.S.A.

FIRST EDITION

QPM   10   9   8   7   6   5   4   3   2   1

Special Thanks

A lot of hard-working people are responsible for Rebecca's Garden. But the one person who really made it happen is Jay, my husband. Without his support at home, work, and with the kids, there would be no Rebecca's Garden on television or in a book. To him I'm most grateful. He stuck with me so I could pursue a dream. To Jay, thank you! You've been a great father . . . and, in the last two years, a great mother to our children.

I'm also very fortunate to have a fabulously talented staff wrapped around the show. To everyone at Hearst-Argyle Television Productions, a big thank you: Producers, Lori Fink Garelick and Katie Beirne Toulmin; Associate Producers, Mary Clarke and Darren Howelton; Art Director, Jane Funke Holland; Hair/Makeup/Wardrobe, Denice Lacher; Videographer, Ian Logan; Audio, Mike Severson and Rosemary Ann Davis; On-line Editor, Scott Shucher; Off-line Editors, David Eells and Barry Mullin; Operations Manager, Ted Perzan; Business Administrator, Melissa Martin; Production Assistant, Nikki Kapurch; VP/GM HBP, Bruce Marson; Horticultural Advisor, Mike Hibbard. And to Gil Maurer and Fred Young, thank you so much for your vision and support.

A thank-you to my editor, Jennifer Sawyer Fisher, who planted the seed to get the book growing; and to Robin Davis-Gomez and Anne Marie Spagnuolo, at Avon Books, for making sure every detail of this book was perfect.

To the deal maker, my agent, Mendes Napoli, thank you.

To Dawn Duffy, thanks for keeping my life in order and for the many contributions and research you have done for this book.

And finally, to two of the most adorable children in the world, Taylor and Madison—I love you all the way to outer space!

*The greatest gift
you can give to someone
is the gift to garden.*

Contents

Introduction

I don't know everything about gardening—I wish I did. No, I take that back—knowing everything is boring! Learning is exciting, challenging, and gives you something to look forward to. And that's what gardening is all about.

I've been digging in the dirt as long as I can remember. There was even a period in my life when I savored the taste of soil. Yes, I was a kid who salivated for soil! From my young experimentation, the best-tasting dirt came from the sandy hills of Sunnyside, Utah, where my grandparents lived. I spent many summer months terrorizing my grandparents, as any young kid would. I looked forward to picking bluebells off the beaten path, savoring my grandmother's chicken and dumplings—the best in the world—and tinkering in the very organized and beautiful backyard garden. My love for flowers came from my dad's mother. She grew the most beautiful flowers. I could easily spend hours on end running and hiding in between the towering blooms of beauty. Life was good back then—but little did I realize how simple down-to-the-earth activities would have such an impact on me as I grew older. That "digging thing" was a blast. Getting dirty without getting in trouble! What more could I ask for? At home my parents continued to instill a love for the land. Our vacations were always spent in a camper perched high in the mountains. We fished, hunted, and played in some of the most beautiful terrain in America. Isolated, we talked a lot. We had "pure" fun. Not until I grew older and wiser did I appreciate the gift my parents and grandparents were passing on to me.

Funny thing, now I want my kids to experience the same thing as I did. But life is so busy now. The only way to bring me and my family back in touch with the simple things is nature. When my kids were tiny babies, they were strapped into a backpack and carried through the woods and gardens of the Rockies. They love living in the great outdoors. My son once said to my husband, "Daddy, can we camp forever?" That's what nature does—that's what gardening does. I want everyone to experience it.

Gardening can be and sometimes is intimidating. But you just have to do it! And that's the intention of this book: simple ideas and tips to get you started, get you excited, and get you outdoors. It won't teach you the ABCs of gardening—there are enough books out there to do that. Instead I hope it inspires you to have fun and to just go out there and get your hands dirty!

Rebecca Kolls

Before You
Get Started

Choose the
Right Tools

If you've ever shopped for gardening tools, you know the large variety of tools available makes it a daunting task. But what do you really need to get started? Here are the basics. Every gardener needs a good shovel and a good rake. For either, the first thing to consider is the handle. Remember, the longer the handle the easier the digging and the happier your back will be. Also, the hardware is very important. Look where the metal attaches to the handle. This is called the shank. Try to find tools with a closed shank. Open shanks are more likely to let water and mud get to the wood and eventually cause rotting. The blade of the shovel or spade should be thick. And the footstep should be bent at a 90-degree angle. Many footsteps are curved and are hard on your feet as you push the shovel into the ground.

The same rules generally apply when buying a rake. In addition, try to find a rake that has a flat back. This gives you versatility. Not only can you weed, cultivate, and aerate, but also the flat side of the rake is great for leveling off the soil in your garden.

Another basic garden tool is the trowel. It comes in all shapes and sizes. But to start, buy one with a wider blade, preferably stainless steel. Stainless steel doesn't rust, bend, or break. Also, trowels with cushioned handles soften the blows to your hands when the going gets tough!

Another gardening staple is pruning shears. You don't want to cut corners on price. It's important to buy a quality pair of shears. With proper care, they'll last a lifetime. I prefer what's called bypass pruning shears. They work like small household scissors. The design allows the blade to make a clean cut and not crush the stem. The blades can be sharpened when needed.

Finally, don't forget gloves. I usually don't wear gloves but when I do, goatskin can't be beat. Goatskin gloves fit snugly, protect your hands, don't allow even the smallest particles through, and last a long time.

These tools will help you get started. As your garden grows your tool collection will grow according to your needs.

Understand Your Dirt-y Duty

Gardening is like building a house. The most important part is a good founda-tion. Your garden's foundation is the soil. Many people try to save money by not improving their soil. Those same people rush to spend hundreds of dollars on plants. Later in the season they scratch their heads and wonder why the plants died or just don't look right. Word to the wise: If you're on a limited budget, spend it on building your soil first.

After reading this part, I realized that perhaps we should start with terms and how they're used. Many seem interchange-able, but they're not.

You'll often come across terms such as "organic matter," "compost," "humus," and "loam." Here's what they mean:

Organic matter: This is what you get after a plant dies. It includes any mate-rial that was once living: trees, vegeta-bles, flowers, shrubs, bones, nuts, etc. This material is typically too large and chunky to mix into the garden soil.

Compost: This is what you get when the organic matter breaks down and is mixed with various plants, soil, air, and water. The final product looks like soil with bits and pieces of dead plant mate-rial. It's loaded with nutrients.

Humus: This is compost that has been allowed to decompose to a fine silky texture.

Loam: This is a soil type typically containing equal parts of sand, silt, and clay—every gardener's dream. Loam can be achieved with the help of compost.

There are three different types of

soil: clay, sand, and loam. Clay soil is the worst as far as I'm concerned. Unimproved clay soil is like cement. It suffocates plants. Grab some cow manure, peat moss, and compost to start. Twice each year, in the spring and fall, mix each of these with the clay. It will take a couple of years, but eventually this will make a huge difference and give you a healthier garden.

Sandy soil is just the opposite. Sand has lots of open spaces that allow water to drain rapidly—too rapidly. This washes away vital nutrients for your garden. Again, mix in the three magic ingredients: cow manure, peat moss, and compost. Add these twice a year and you will reap a bountiful harvest from your garden.

Then there's loam. You're lucky to be at heaven's gate. Still, you'll need to replenish loam with cow manure, peat moss, and compost. These three will ensure that your healthy soil will stay that way over time. All garden centers should have these three products. You can also check city compost sites or visit your best friend, the farmer, and offer to take or buy some manure off his hands. Fresh manure should always be added in the fall so it has time to break down. If applied in the spring, it might burn your plants. Remember, be generous. Spread a nice thick layer of your amendment mixture throughout your garden. The layer should be at least 2 to 3 inches. Add more if you can. You can't just leave it on the soil sur-face. In order for it to do its job it must be mixed into the soil. The deeper you can mix it, particularly for new gardens, annuals, and vegetables, the better. But for most annual gardens mixing at the depth of at least six inches will be effective. Do this in the spring and again in the fall and soon you'll see, feel, and smell the benefits of great soil. Make it routine to amend your soil every year. This is your way of giving back to the earth.

Start from the Ground Up

Wait! Stop! Before you run out into your soggy spring garden, you must read this: Digging, scraping, and turning over the soil too early can have disastrous results. People get anxious to turn the soil and their timing is often bad. What timing? You can't wait to dig, right? Working with wet soil creates dirt clods that dry almost as hard as cement. Stay away from the garden if the soil is too wet. Easy to say, but how do you know when it's too wet? Grab a handful of soil and squish it into a ball. Gently toss the ball of soil in your hand (toss it up about 4 to 6 inches) and flatten your hand so the mud ball makes a firm impact with your palm. If the ball of soil breaks apart, you're ready to break your back by doing some digging! If the ball doesn't break apart, the soil is too wet. Wait a week and try the test again.

Know Your Zone

Before you start sinking plants in the garden there is something you should know—your zone! The country is divided up according to average minimum temperatures in the winter. Zone 1 includes those areas with the coldest winters, zone 11 the warmest. Each zone represents a 10°F difference. Find the zone where you live and remember it. This comes in handy, especially if you let your fingers do the walking through mail-order catalogues.

Believe me, I've learned the hard way. I ordered a beautiful flower from Seattle. I couldn't wait to see what it would look like in my garden, located clear across the country. I laboriously planted it. Coddled it through the winds and rain. Then winter came. That was the last time I saw that plant. It was in the wrong zone. As you choose your plants, look on the label. The zone should be listed. If the plant is hardy in zones 4 to 7 and you live in zone 5, you're set. But if you live in zone 3 the plant will probably die from the cold temperatures. And one more thing: If you live on a hill or mountain or down in the valley your zone will be altered—cool air pools in lower-lying areas whereas hilltops heat up faster—be careful.

Rebecca's Garden

Spring

. . . the planting season

Spring—saved at last! Don't get me wrong, I love winter. I love how it looks, how it smells, how it feels, and I especially love it when it's over! Spring brings hope, revival, life—and color!

It must be something in the air. Warmer weather works like an infusion of adrenaline. People get an inexplicable urge to dig, rake, and plant. Too bad we can't capture and bottle some of that energy for summer.

So shall we dig in? Let's get those hands dirty!

Vegetable Gardens

GETTING STARTED

Pick a Site

The perfect space has eight to ten hours of sunlight. It's flat or slightly sloped to the south. Avoid slopes or hills that are too steep, because heavy rain could wash away your crops. And of course, keep your garden within easy reach of your home to simplify watering chores.

If you live in a place with less sunlight, don't be discouraged. You still have plenty of options. Choose vegetables that thrive in shady, cooler locations. I enjoy a variety of lettuce, carrots, and beets. They all do well in places that get at least four hours of sunlight.

There are things to avoid in your garden that are usually your friends in any other place. Believe it or not, trees pose a threat to your vegetable garden's vitality. The roots of trees suck up the soil nutrients your garden needs to grow. Trees also compete for water—and because they're bigger they usually win the water war with your vegetables.

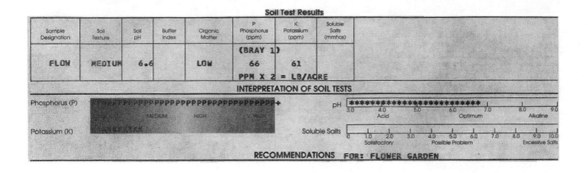

Soil Test Results								
Sample Designation	Soil Texture	Soil pH	Buffer Index	Organic Matter	P Phosphorus (ppm)	K Potassium (ppm)	Soluble Salts (mmhos)	
FLOW	MEDIUM	6.6		LOW	(BRAY 1) 66	61		
					PPM X 2 = LB/ACRE			

INTERPRETATION OF SOIL TESTS

Phosphorus (P)

Potassium (K)

pH

Soluble Salts

RECOMMENDATIONS FOR: FLOWER GARDEN

Create a Plan

Avoid headaches down the road by planning ahead. The beautiful thing is there are no set rules. The most important part of the plan is space. Leave yourself enough room to work in and around the plants in your garden. One idea I love is mixing vegetables among flowers and herbs for a potpourri of color and texture. It's unexpected, but attractive and functional.

Walking is great, but not for your garden. Don't spend a lot of time walking in your garden because it compacts the soil and suffocates your plants.

THE SOIL

Get a Test

Now you need a report card on your soil's performance. I strongly suggest you contact your local cooperative extension service. Extension services have soil testing kits and can explain how they work. Basically, you grab a small sample of soil from five different locations in your garden. Mix it up. Put it in a bag. Then send it in to the extension service. They'll give your soil an evaluation. The so-called "report card" will tell you what you need to do to make your soil better for growing. I highly recommend this test. It will save you a lot of time and lost vegetation. It might even save your garden.

This test measures the soil's fertility and tells you which nutrients are out of balance or lacking. It also measures the soil's pH, which goes from 0 to 14. Anything between 6 and 7 is considered ideal. In addition to measurements that describe the current state of your soil, the test supplies recommendations. These tell you what and how much material you need to add to boost its grade.

Improve the Soil

I know you've probably just put in a long week at work or in your home. But you still want to have the best garden imaginable, right? So stay away from the lemonade and the shade for now. What I'm about to tell you isn't light work, but it's essential for your new garden.

The absolute best way of building your soil is a technique called double digging. It's good for more than just vegetable gardens. It's a method you should also use for perennial beds and for any other areas with plants that will not be replaced each year.

Start off by removing any existing sod and digging a trench. It should be about 6 to 8 inches deep. The soil you dig out from the first trench should be set aside in a wheelbarrow; you'll need it again shortly. Then in the same trench, dig down another 6 to 8 inches and loosen the soil. Don't remove it. Spread about four inches of combined peat moss, rotted manure, and compost on top. Now move to trench number 2. Start the process all over again, but this time as you dig out the soil in number 2, throw it into the first trench. This should bring the soil level to the top of the first trench. (If not, add more organic material to make it level.) Turn the soil and organic matter in trench number 1 with the shovel to mix it together. The first trench is done. Do this same routine for the rest of the trenches; use the soil in the wheelbarrow to fill the last trench. That's double digging!

If double digging isn't for you, rototilling is the next best option. A

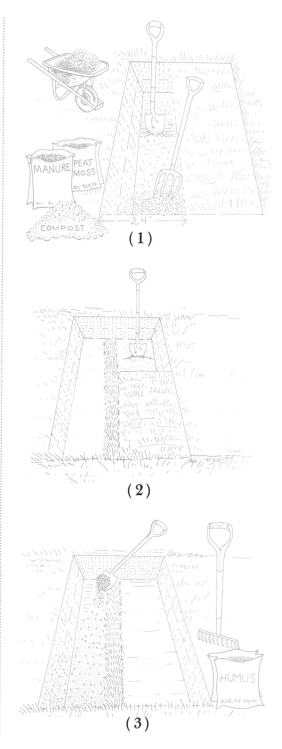

(1)

(2)

(3)

rototiller can be rented from most hardware stores. To start, remove all sod or grass. If you don't it will grow back after tilling. Then cover the garden area with a generous layer of organic material such as peat moss, rotted manure, humus, or compost. With the tiller, mix in the amendments to a depth of at least 6 inches.

PLANTING

Not all vegetables are the same. Some take the entire growing season to mature, while others do it in half the time. Some like the cool weather but explode with growth when it gets warm. Some are planted from seeds while others are transplanted. As you begin your vegetable garden adventure, you'll learn the different conditions in which plants thrive. The key to successful vegetable gardens is to give each vegetable the amount of space it needs to get the job done, and to give them the right amount of sun, water, and nutrition. The best we can hope for is that the sun will shine—a lot! Water can be controlled. If you don't get a good rain once a week, you'll have to supply the water for the plants. It's really important to have a good watering schedule and stick with it. Typically most plants will appreciate about an inch of water a week.

Plants also like to be fed. If you enrich the garden in the spring prior to planting, the vegetables will be off to a good start. Then most vegetables will thrive with applications of an all-purpose 10-10-10 fertilizer every three to four weeks either scratched into the soil (side-dress) or watered in with a liquid fertilizer.

To help you get started, here are five easy vegetables to plant that are bound to build your vegetable-growing confidence:

Peas: Peas love cool weather and can be planted in spring as soon as the soil is dry enough to work. Like most vegetables, they grow best in rich, well cultivated soil. Full sun is best, but peas will tolerate some shade. Two weeks before planting, mix an all-purpose fertilizer into the soil. Peas grow best vertically on netting or a trellis, which should be set up before you start planting. Soak seeds overnight for quicker germination. Then plant the seeds in double rows. Within each row, plant seeds 1 to 2 inches deep, 3 to 6 inches apart. Space the set of rows 2 feet from each other.

You'll know the peas are ready for harvest when the pods begin to swell. If you can see an imprint of the peas inside, you've waited too long.

As peas develop, remember this tip: The more you pick, the more the plants produce.

Spring

Beets: Beets are another cool-season vegetable. Beets tolerate most soils and grow well in full sun or part shade. Like peas, beets should be planted as soon as the soil can be worked. Plant beet seeds ½ to 1 inch deep and about 2 inches apart. Each "seed" will actually produce two to three beets. It's important to thin them down to one beet as they grow. Regular watering is important since beets will become tough and woody if the soil dries out.

When the beet is about 2 inches wide (a little bigger than a golfball), it's ready. Gently grasp the base of the greens and pull. Don't throw out the greens, because they're edible. Steam as you would spinach.

Trouble skinning beets? Drop in boiling water for a few minutes to loosen skins.

Broccoli: Broccoli too likes cool weather. It grows well in rich organic soil exposed to full sun, although it will tolerate some shade. This plant doesn't need much attention except a good drink on a regular basis and a shot of fertilizer every three to four weeks. The flowers, the edible part, start growing from the center.

Harvest when the buds on the head are still tightly closed. (If buds start to open, you've waited too long and the head should be picked quickly.) Harvest the head with a sharp knife, cutting about 4 inches of the stem. Once you harvest the one head, continue to water the plant. It will continue to produce small flowerets in the crotches of the stems.

Tomatoes and broccoli are delicacies to cutworms. To prevent your plants from being chomped off at the base place a tuna can without the top and bottom around the plant and push it into the soil, leaving about ¼ inch of the can above the soil.

Cucumbers: Cucumbers are another easy vegetable to grow. I've found it easier to buy transplants from a garden center rather than start plants from seeds. (I like to save seed-starting efforts for the unusual plants generally not found in garden centers.) The cucumber is another warm-season vegetable, so it can't be planted until after the last expected day of frost. Cucumbers prefer rich soil and full sun. Plant them as deeply as they grew in the container. Space each plant about 4 to 6 feet apart— cucumbers like to roam, so give them room. They need less space if you train them to grow vertically, on a trellis or arbor.

Limit fertilizer for the cucumbers. They prefer high-phosphorus, low-nitrogen fertilizers. Feed when you plant them and again when the vines begin to flower. Like tomatoes, cukes need a regular watering schedule to grow good-quality fruit. If not, the cucumber becomes disfigured and its plants produce less. Harvest when cucumbers are about 6 to 8 inches long for the best flavor. The longer you leave them on the vine, the more their quality deteriorates. Fruit production is also slowed if you leave the cukes on the vine too long.

Tomatoes: Tomatoes are one of the most popular vegetables grown in backyard gardens. The flavor from a fresh-picked tomato is unlike that of any store-bought one. Tomatoes can be started indoors from seeds ten weeks before the last frost. However, I would recommend buying transplants from a garden center. You'll save yourself a few headaches. Tomatoes are a warm-season crop, which means they can't be planted until all threat of frost is gone. They grow best in loose, fertile soil and full sun. In the garden, dig two holes 18 to 36 inches apart. The rows should be 3 feet apart.

One hole is for the plant, the other for a small handful of an all-purpose 10-10-10 fertilizer. (See explanation of fertilizer packaging on p. 48.) Plant the tomato as deeply as possible, up to the first cluster of leaves. Roots will develop on the buried portion of stem. Fill each hole with soil. Plants should be spaced about 2 to 3 feet apart. Good air circulation is very important for growing healthy plants. If plants are too close they're more susceptible to blight.

Tomatoes love water. Too much is better than too little (but too wet is not good either). The key is to be consistent especially when the fruit is ripening. If the plants experience a sudden fluctuation or change in moisture, the tomato will crack or develop a brown leathery bruise on the bottom of the fruit. This is a common disorder called "blossom-end rot."

Mulch soil when the temperatures rise.

Tomatoes are ready to be picked when they turn from pink to red. Gently twist from vine.

> *Tomatoes lose their flavor in the refrigerator. Keep them on the kitchen counter to retain the "just picked from the vine" flavor.*

Plastic Greenhouses to Extend Your Growing Season

I live in Wisconsin, the frozen tundra of the States, next to Canada. It can get very cold up here! And it can stay cold for a long time. The warm-season crops can't

go into the ground until after Memorial Day. Then the first nip of frost usually strikes sometime during the first couple of weeks in October—not a long growing season. So we Northern Plains people are always looking for devices to extend the growing season.

One product that works especially well on tomatoes is the "Wall-O'-Waters." A Wall-O'-Waters is nothing more than a 2-ply plastic teepee. The tent is divided into cylinders, which you fill with water. The tent is placed over one tomato plant, like a miniature greenhouse. The daytime sun heats up the water. The heat is captured in the water-filled tubes and keeps the plant warm at night. It also protects the plant from a late frost. With Wall-O'-Waters I can

plant my tomatoes one month earlier—which means I'm picking ripe tomatoes before anyone else!

STEP-BY-STEP:
INSTALLING A
WALL-O'-WATERS

- *Plant tomato*
- *Cover with 5-gallon bucket*
- *Place empty Wall-O'-Waters over bucket*
- *Fill each cylinder three-quarters full with water*
- *Remove bucket*
- *Squeeze top together, forming a teepee around the tomato*

As the daytime temperatures climb, you'll have to open the water tent to keep the plant from overheating. The easiest way to do this is to top off the water in each tube. If you fill the tubes full (rather than three-quarters full), the walls will naturally stand erect. The tent can stay on the plant until about one month after the last frost date. Then collapse the Wall-O'-Waters by squeezing the water out. Remove the Wall-O'-Waters by lifting it over the top of the plant. And don't throw it out; Wall-O'-Waters are reusable.

Too many aphids? Control them with ladybugs! Order from garden centers or mail-order catalogs.

PEST MANAGEMENT

Gardens are a magnet for insects with voracious appetites. If you don't watch it, they'll clean out the crops before you can. So it's important to stay ahead of the game. Every couple of days plan an insect hunt. Look closely at the top of each plant and pay particular attention to the underside of the plant's leaves. You're looking for creepy crawling things, small sacs, or eggs. If you spot these pick them off. Many insects take a special liking to particular plants. Try to learn to identify these insects and the plants they like best. It makes your inspection much easier. If the insects are winning the battle, it's time to pull out the hose. A sharp stream of water does wonders. If that doesn't do the trick, try insecticidal soap. This is a safe product to spray on your plants. Be sure to spray each plant on top and underneath its leaves.

Here's a recipe for home-made insecticidal soap: Mix 1 to 3 tablespoons of dishwashing liquid into 1 gallon water. Test a small portion of the plant before spraying it completely. Some plants will be sensitive to the soap and will easily burn. If no injury shows in a day or two, saturate the tops and bottoms of all leaves. Insecticidal soap is excellent for controlling small insects.

Nature's Black Gold

Some of my fondest memories are of days spent at my grandparents' house. They had a beautiful backyard garden. I loved to get my hands dirty digging in it. As a kid, I thought my grandparents were a little crazy because they used to make me carry out what I thought were odd chores in the garden. They would save all their kitchen scraps in a big bowl. After each meal it was my duty to take them to the "garbage" pile. It was a nasty job and I thought they must have done something pretty bad to have the garbageman boycott their home.

But that wasn't the only odd job. Grandma would wash her dishes in a big tin tub that fit nicely in the sink. Instead of pouring the gray water down the drain, she would get me to dump it at the base of trees and shrubs. I was convinced that they were too stingy with money to use clean water. And as if that wasn't enough, when vegetables were steamed, potatoes boiled, or pasta cooked the water was given to me. I went begrudgingly off to the flower beds with this stuff. I was convinced they were crazy. Little did I know they were politically and organically correct. While most of us were running for the synthetic stuff, pest controls included, they stayed home and gave back only the natural stuff. That was a big lesson for me. It is because of their "weird" behavior that I am a gardener who now practices what they preached for years.

Probably the most memorable event in their garden took place when Grandpa explained the "garbage" pile to me. He made me put my arm into the pile. Shocked by its heat, I pulled my hand out quickly. "You see, my dear, the wheel of life is turning in that pile," he said in the most passionate way. Picking up the humus he said, "Here's how we can repay the earth for all the wonderful things we get from it. We must not be selfish, we must always give something back." And now I always do. I always find room for a "garbage" pile.

HOW COMPOSTING WORKS

Composting is not as complicated as it might seem. It happens every day on the forest floor. It's Mother Nature's way of renewing the earth. And for your garden it's black gold. Creating a compost pile is simple. It can be as easy as heaping kitchen parings and yard trimmings in a pile or it can be quite sophisticated. Either way the goal is to avoid heaping more garbage into landfills. The idea is to recycle as much as possible.

Striking it rich requires a simple recipe of layering wet and dry materials. Wet materials (referred to as "green") include grass clippings, kitchen scraps, manure, and coffee grounds. The drier "brown" materials consist of autumn leaves, straw or hay, fine shrub trimmings, shredded newspaper, sawdust, hair, dryer lint, wood ashes, etc. When you combine the wet with the dry, along with a couple shovelfuls of soil, a magical thing happens. Tiny microorganisms in the soil begin working away, breaking down all the materials. As they work, they generate heat. To stay alive, the bacteria need moisture. So it's important to keep the compost pile damp, but not wet. Another important ingredient is oxygen; it helps the decomposition process. So it's important to supply the necessary oxygen throughout the pile. You can do that by stirring the pile every few days, therefore making sure enough air gets mixed into the pile to keep it cooking. A good compost pile will heat up to 100° or 150°F. When the process is complete the compost will cool down. That's a good indication your pile is done or that it's time to turn the pile again. When the pile is cool and looks like rich, dark soil, the cycle is finished.

HOW TO MAKE COMPOST

The easiest method is a simple pile. Another method involves one or

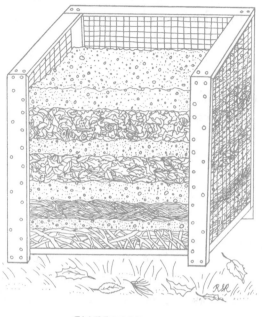

INTERIOR

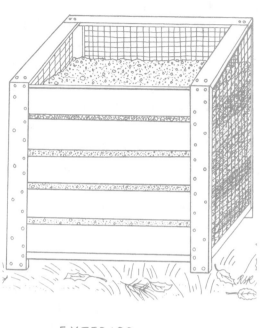

EXTERIOR

more cages. Round or four-sided cages confine the compost and keep it neatly tucked in. If you have more than one cage, you can build another pile while the first is decomposing.

The frames are usually made out of wood with chicken wire or wire mesh used for the caging. Typical dimensions are 3×3×3 or 4×4×4.

Place large materials on the bottom of the pile. Large sticks crossed over each other work well. This will prevent the bottom layers from compacting. It also aids in drainage. Then begin layering the green and brown material. Between each layer add a shovelful of soil. Continue layering. Then top off your pile with a layer of soil thick enough to cover the pile 1 to 2 inches. This keeps the decomposing material contained, bad smells and all.

Every few days mix the concoction. If the pile is dry, spray some water over the heap with the garden hose. But typically Mother Nature does a pretty good job of keeping the pile perfectly moist. If the pile smells sour, it's too wet or too green. You must open up the pile and allow the materials to dry out. This happens if you use a lot of grass clippings without mixing them with brown materials. You'll know the pile is working if it's warm or hot to the touch in the center. It will continue to be warm until all the material is broken down or decomposed (or until it needs mixing). When it begins cooling, the transformation is done. The whole process can take three to four weeks, depending on the size of the pile. Think of compost as the garden fixer. It feeds plants, it helps build good, healthy soil, and it can be used as a mulch. Anytime you're digging, add compost. And if you have too much, make a pile and plant pumpkins or squash on it.

Composting in a Can

For those who may not have the space or the material for a large compost pile, here's an idea. Buy a large black plastic garbage can, one with a tight lid (the black color will help heat the compost). With a knife or sharp shears, very carefully remove the bottom. Then drill holes randomly around the sides of the can. The holes should be no larger than 1 inch. This will allow air to get in and out of the compost. Find a sunny spot to place your can. Then layer the can by filling it up with your plant debris and kitchen scraps. To keep the contents mixed, every week or so simply lift the can. Don't worry about weight; the decomposing materials will fall out of the bottom. Move the can over to a clean spot and refill it with the same debris, mixing as you go. Within weeks you'll start to see the transformation.

Materials for the Heap

GOOD	BAD
Clean grass clippings	Grass that's been chemically treated
Cow, horse, turkey, rabbit, goat, sheep manure	Dog or cat manure
Hair clippings—human and dog	Meat scraps
Shredded newspaper	Plastics
All fruit and vegetable kitchen scraps	Magazines or colored paper
Coffee grounds	Charcoal ashes
Eggshells	Fish products
Sawdust	Diseased plant material
Wood ashes	Perennial weeds
Autumn leaves	Grandma's false teeth
Seed hulls	

Flower Gardens

Your next stop at the floral shop could literally be as close as your own backyard. With some planning and a little homework you can have blooms ready for picking any time of the season.

You must start with the soil. Enrich it with the three magic ingredients: peat moss, manure, and compost. It will pay off in a big way as the flowers sound their symphony of color. The perennial garden especially needs a lot of attention before you sink any stock. Since these plants will be in one location year after year, it's important to get in and enrich the soil before they're planted. Double digging is the answer (see page 5).

Garden in the clouds! Cloudy, gray days are better for planting flowers and vegetables. The plants are less likely to suffer from transplanting shock. Sunny, hot days cause new plants to wilt quickly.

ANNUALS VS. PERENNIALS

To get started let's begin with the basics. Most people refer to flowers mainly by two groups, annuals and perennials. Annuals are those flowers that grow, bloom, set seeds, and die all in one season. They must be replaced every year. Perennials bloom every year, die back in the winter, and come back the next spring.

ANNUALS

To me annuals are a must, as they provide the backbone of continuous color in the garden. They work especially well in perennial gardens to fill in the gaps, and to supply color while perennials aren't blooming. Annuals are either started from seeds or purchased as transplants from the garden center. They're usually bought in containers called cell packs. Many people pop out the brick of flowers and plant the whole thing. However, each brick usually contains at least four to six flowers so they can be divided. Very carefully tease the brick apart into separate plants. The roots, if tangled together, should be loosened or gently teased apart. This helps the roots stretch out in search of food and water.

Planting

Never plant your flowers deeper than they grew in their container. You might want to mix a slow-release fertilizer into the soil prior to planting. Then you're done fertilizing, as this special type of fertilizer will continue to feed your plants for you all season long. If you use ordinary fertilizer, lightly fertilize initially and then every three to four weeks use half-strength liquid fertilizer or scratch a little all-purpose fertilizer (10-10-10) into the soil.

To keep your annual flowers looking spectacular all season long, you must deadhead. That's a nice way of saying behead your flowers as they are fading and before they set seeds. An annual flower's goal is to make seeds. Once it makes seeds, the plant quits using energy to make any more blooms—it has accomplished its mission. Removing the blooms keeps the flowers coming. For the tiny masses of flowers like sweet alyssum, lobelia, and pansies, a good cut in midsummer will pay off in the fall. Such flowers will send out a new flush of blooms lasting right through the first frost. If the plant does set seeds, you might want to try saving the seeds for next year's flowers.

I don't like wearing gloves unless I absolutely have to. The drawback is dirt under my nails. Here's an old trick. Before digging in the dirt, dig your nails into a bar of soap. The soap gets under the nail so the dirt can't! When you finish in the yard, wash your hands and watch the soap dissolve, leaving you with clean nails.

Here are some popular and easy to grow annuals. They don't need a lot of attention, they're not fussy about soils, and they don't battle with many pests or diseases.

Sweet Alyssum: This is one of my favorite annual flowers. Sweet alyssum is a great edging plant. It grows about 4 inches high and spreads out along the ground. Soft clusters of dainty white, fragrant flowers perfume the air and invite bees. Alyssum is especially effective lining a path or walkway. The white color reflects moonlight and appears to light the way. Sweet alyssum grows quickly, making it a good candidate for window boxes and containers. The blooms come early and stay late. It prefers rich soil but will grow in some of the poorest soil. It does best in full sunshine and appreciates 10-10-10 fertilizer scratched into the soil every three weeks.

> *In the summer when sweet alyssum looks tired, give it a haircut. Shear off the faded blooms in July. Within weeks the plant will be rejuvenated and ready for another profusion of blooms.*

Petunia: One of the most popular annuals in America is the petunia, and for good reason. This is a flower that can take on bad soil, bad weather, and bad attention and still look pretty good. Petunias are low growers, about 10 to 12 inches tall, but the Grandiflora grows up to 16 inches. They come in a rainbow of colors. The "wave" varieties are nothing shy of spectacular. Use them in boxes and containers, as they cascade with colorful blooms. They prefer sun but will tolerate some shade. Without fertilizers they grow and bloom slowly. But a feeding every three weeks will make this flower shine. Clip off the dead blooms to keep petunias from becoming leggy and ragged.

Marigold: If you think you can't grow flowers, here's one that will prove you wrong. Marigolds are truly one of the easiest annuals to grow. They range in height from 6 inches to 3 feet. Their colors are mostly golden—yellows, oranges, and some mixed with red. They thrive in sunny, hot locations and, if you can believe this, they'd rather have rotten soil than rich soil! Plant in spring after all threat of frost is gone. Pinch off the first set of buds to encourage bushier plants. Marigolds put on their best display from midsummer to frost. Cut off spent flowers to assure more blooms.

Impatiens: If you have shade to contend with, then this is the flower you need. Impatiens do a beautiful job adding color to an otherwise dreary corner. White impatiens are especially effective for adding light. Impatiens are considered perennials but are killed by frost. They're grown in most places as an annual. They start out as a small plant but quickly reach a height of 6 to 18 inches depending on the variety. They are low maintenance flowers and don't have many disease or insect problems. The colors range from white, red, pink, and purple to orange. Impatiens are very sensitive to cold nights, so wait until all danger of frost is gone before planting. Most impatiens prefer shade although the New Guinea types tolerate more sun. All impatiens are heavy drinkers. Keep them moist and fertilize regularly—once every three to four weeks.

Coleus: Got a boring corner? Bring it alive with coleus. This plant is a new one for me, but I'm sold on it. I was once given a flat of these flowers and I sank them into a mulch-covered mound only for it to become the talk of the town. This plant is not a favorite for its tiny flowers (which should be pinched off) but for its extraordinary foliage. Leaves come in vivid shades and mixtures of green, pink, red, maroon, creamy yellow, and white. It ranges in height from 6 to 36 inches. This plant produces the best color in shade to partial sun, as the color will fade if it gets too much sun. Coleus will not tolerate a nip of frost so wait until after any danger of frost before planting. Pinch off branch tips throughout the season to encourage bushier plants. Water and feed regularly.

Sunflower: If you have kids, you have to make room for sunflowers. This is as close to Jack's beanstalk as it gets. Planted from seeds in the spring, sunflowers germinate quickly and grow just as fast. They obviously love the sun and tolerate any kind of soil. The largest sunflowers grow up to 15 feet. The colossal heads fill with seeds that make a tasty treat at the end of the season. Wait until all danger of frost has passed before planting seeds in spring. Water well and fertilize every three to four weeks. Harvest heads when they become brown and dry.

Pansy: Don't let the name fool you on this flower. Pansies are one of the toughest annuals when it comes to cooler weather. They bring color early and again late into the season. And if you live in an area that barely goes below 32°F, you may be treated with flowers all winter long. Pansies like moist soil and lots of fertilizer. They grow best, and last longer, in partial sun. For containers or window boxes fill with a soil mix that contains plenty of peat moss. As the season warms up, cut the plants in half and mulch around the base. By fall you'll be treated to a second bloom.

Zinnia: Whatever you're trying to achieve in the flower garden, the zinnia can help you. This is a versatile flower that comes in all sizes and colors. It's a must for the cutting garden. Zinnias will tolerate all kinds of soil and truly love the heat. Wait to plant them until after all danger of frost has passed. Once they're planted that's it. No pinching, no deadheading. They'll do the rest and grow 12 to 32 inches in height. Just be careful with the water; zinnias like it on the dry side. They appreciate fertilizer every three to four weeks.

Verbena: Like impatiens, this is a tender perennial grown as an annual. This one thrives in hot, dry areas. It has tiny blossom clusters that are perched on top of spindly green stems. Verbenas bloom early and continue to display flowers throughout the season. They vary in size but usually grow 8 to 15 inches tall. The colors range from red, pink, white, cream, coral, and purple to rose. There are trailing types that work best in containers and window boxes. Take it easy on the water as verbenas aren't heavy drinkers. Fertilize every three to four weeks.

Snapdragon: Of all flowers snapdragons tend to conjure up childhood memories. The dragon-like face with the moving jaw was always fun to play with. But for the grower, it's the vast range of colors and heights that make this a favorite.

Snapdragons can be started from seed indoors 10 to 12 weeks before the last frost, or they can be purchased as transplants. They like the cool weather and will tolerate light frosts. Plant them when the soil is dry enough and about two weeks before the last frost. They prefer sunny locations and will bloom early summer to mid-fall. They range in colors from white, yellow, pink, purple, rose, orange, and scarlet, to lavender. Height ranges from 6 to 36 inches. They are great for flower arrangements since they last so long.

PERENNIALS

Perennials are a great addition to any garden since maintenance is minimal. Their only drawback is they don't bloom all season long, only a few weeks. So as you plan your perennial garden you must choreograph plants so you have a succession of blooms. For the die-hard gardeners, perennials can be started from seeds, but you're looking at a laborious process. (Some take two years to bloom from seeds.)

Buy transplants. Enrich the soil very deeply. If you dig deep when preparing the soil, it shouldn't need digging for about five years. After enriching soil throughout the planting area, dig a planting hole as deep as the container and double its width. Next, mix in a slow-release fertilizer. Remove the plant from its container and loosen the roots by making three or four shallow cuts with a knife or trowel into the sides and bottom of the root ball. Place the plant in the hole and fill halfway with soil; fill with water and allow it to drain. Finish filling in soil, water well, and mulch to reduce weeds.

Have patience with perennials; it takes time for them to look full and fabulous. Remember, the first year they sleep, the second year they creep, and the third year they leap.

Double Your Flower Assets by Division

You hear it all the time—perennials are described as the "low-maintenance" flowers. But what I'm about to tell you won't seem low maintenance at all. It's a technique called dividing. And as much as you might like to avoid it, it's the best way to keep your perennial flowers healthy and looking great. Not convinced yet? Look at it this way. There are kickbacks: As you divide, you'll double or triple the number of plants you can add to your garden at no extra cost!

Dividing is done by digging up the clump and pulling it apart at the roots. Sounds a tad dramatic, but that's what you do. Most plants are divided in the early spring, but some prefer division in the late summer or fall. If you're dividing plant clumps with dead centers, cut out all the dead material before transplanting. Once you've divided the plant it should be replanted right away.

Don't forget to enrich the soil before planting.

For plants with smaller tough clumping roots such as ornamental grasses, drive the blade of a sharp shovel through the roots. Or get out the axe and start swinging. One quick swing and one plant becomes two.

Fleshy-rooted plants such as peonies and iris can be cut with a knife. Just be sure each division has a clump of leaves or buds on it.

Ten Easy Perennials to Get You Started

Most perennials are easy to grow, but here are my top ten based on hardiness, disease resistance, and maintenance.

Daylily: Here is one perennial that's nearly foolproof. Most varieties flourish in any area from sun to nearly full shade. Daylilies are not picky about the soil and are virtually pest free! The large, trumpet-shaped flowers come in many colors

To make matters worse, there are different techniques for division. It all depends on the plant. Look at the roots of the plant you just dug up. If it has large, densely tangled roots like daylilies, insert two garden forks back to back in the center of the plant. Drive them down into the roots and pry them apart. The plant is then doubled.

and hang above tall, wide, grassy foliage. The blooms last only one day, hence the name. Daylilies prefer fertile, well-drained soil and do especially well in hot, dry conditions. Some have fragrant blossoms especially the yellow 'Hyperion.'

Having a luncheon? Daylily flowers are edible and make a beautiful natural bowl for fresh berries.

Bearded Iris: Irises have been beautifying gardens for centuries. This old-fashioned flower is known for its distinctive flowers and lance-shaped foliage. Unfortunately the flower, which blooms in early summer, doesn't last very long. But the light green leaves add a nice background and texture to the garden. Iris loves sunshine and rich, well-drained loamy soil, although this hardy perennial also tolerates dry conditions. If you have heavy clay soil, be careful not to bury the rhizome; leave its top barely exposed.

Spurge (Euphorbia): Spurge is unlike any other flower. In fact it doesn't look like a flower at all. The "flowers" are really colored leaves, or bracts. It grows best in well-drained soil. One of the nicest is cushion spurge. It grows 12 to 18 inches high and has yellow flower bracts above the foliage during the spring. Cushion spurge has an added bonus. In the fall the green foliage turns

blazing red. This flower is extremely drought tolerant. The deer don't like it, nor do the small animals. Be careful handling any spurge, as all have a milky sap that can irritate the skin.

Astilbe: A great plant, astilbe is made for the shade with just a couple hours of sunshine. The flowers of astilbe are soft feathery plumes, which gracefully arch over the fernlike foliage. They grow 8 inches to 4 feet. Astilbe prefers moist, rich well-drained soil. A feeding every three to four weeks while it's blooming will keep this perennial in top shape. Most bloom mid to late summer.

Delphinium: This flower is fast becoming one of my favorites in the perennial garden. Delphinium is an old classic and a must for traditional English-style gardens. It is related to the annual larkspur. Most are tall with stately spikes of color. But there are smaller-flowered larkspur-style varieties, which are great for the cutting garden. All need a rich, moist, but well-drained soil and full sun. Delphiniums do not like the wind. They are heavy feeders. Fertilize with 10-10-10 in spring and again after it blooms. Dead-head faded flowers to encourage repeat blooming.

Peony: This flower is a classic old-fashioned flower favorite for late spring. It's prized for large satiny flowers, which are superb for cutting and dry beautifully in silica sand (found in craft stores). The foliage remains attractive all season, particularly when supported. Peonies prefer a deep, rich, well-drained loamy soil and full sun. New plants take several years to become established and will grow 3 feet tall and spread 3 feet wide. Unlike most perennials, peonies don't like being disturbed; they need to be divided only every ten years. Fertilize plants in the early spring and again after flowering. In the early spring, stake plant to keep top-heavy blooms off the ground. Early in the spring season sink a tomato case, or something similar, into the soil around the emerging plant.

Bleeding-heart: Look closely and you'll see where this plant gets its name. Its rosy, heart-shaped flowers look like a bleeding heart. The flowers hang delicately from horizontally arched stems. The foliage is slightly grayish green with deeply cut leaves. This plant prefers moist, well-drained soil rich in organic matter, partial shade, and no wind. Look for blooms from May to June. This one is great for the cutting garden and it grows 1 to 3 feet tall. Water abundantly and feed regularly. Scratch in a 10-10-10 fertilizer in the spring, then every four weeks.

Yarrow: Yarrow loves the heat and tolerates dry conditions—two elements that make this flower appealing. Yarrow is known for its flat-topped clusters of flowers in buttery yellow, cheesy yellow, rosy pink, and some reds. The flowers sit on top of fernlike silver-green foliage and bloom all summer long. Yarrow establishes and spreads quickly. At times the foliage can look weedy. Deadhead to encourage more blooms.

Hosta: No shade garden can be complete without hosta. These plants are an excellent addition to any garden with their fabulous color and texture. They thrive in the shade in moist, rich soil. A few will do just as well in the sun. But not too much sun or it washes out the color, especially on blue-green varieties. Hostas are best known for their foliage. Leaves come in varying colors and mixtures of green, yellow, and creamy white. The lush, leafy clumps range in height from just inches to 3 feet tall. Hostas send up tall spikes of blue or white flowers in late summer; a few varieties have fragrant flowers.

Deep green and blue-green hostas prefer shady locations. Those more yellow-green in color tolerate sunnier locations.

Purple Coneflower (Echinacea): Coneflower has been deemed "Perennial of the Year" for 1998, and with good reason. It's easy to grow, beautiful, and long-blooming. It looks like a giant daisy with a large, protruding brown center cone. Coneflower prefers well-drained soil and must have good drainage during the winter. It grows 24 to 36 inches tall and comes in pinkish rose, creamy white, or purple. Coneflower blooms from mid-summer to fall. The tall blooming stems can get heavy so staking is sometimes necessary to keep plants upright. This flower dries very well. See the section on drying on page 75.

A Symphony of Blooms

The one drawback to perennial flowers is their short blooming period (unlike annual flowers, which bloom all summer long). But with a little homework and some orchestration, you can arrange a symphony of color all season long.

As you're planning your garden, divide the flowers into categories according to blooming time: spring, summer, and fall. Then mix the combinations. That way as one flower stops blooming, another is just preparing to open. Here's the short list of my seasonal categories:

SPRING BLOOMERS

Artemisia 'Silver Mound'
Bleeding-heart
Crocus
Cushion Spurge
Dwarf Iris
Forget-me-not
Jack-in-the-pulpit
Moss Phlox (Phlox subulata)
Trillium
Virginia Bluebells

SUMMER BLOOMERS

Astilbe
Baby's-breath (Gypsophila)
Beardtongue (Penstemon)
Bee balm (Monarda)
Bellflower
Black-eyed Susan (Rudbeckia)
Coral Bells
Daylily
Delphinium
Hosta
Iris
Peony
Pinks (Dianthus)
Poppy
Purple Coneflower (Echinacea)
Salvia
Shasta Daisy
Statice (Sea Lavender)
Tickseed (Coreopsis)
Veronica
Yarrow

> *Aster*
>
> *Chrysanthemum*
>
> *Joe-Pye Weed (Eupatorium)*
>
> *Sedum*
>
> *Sneezeweed (Helenium)*
>
> *Toad Lily*

Garden Table Tops

If you're planning a party and want a beautiful theme without crunching your pocketbook, consider a garden party. This allows you to bring the brilliance of the outdoors inside. Here are some ideas:

Place markers: Purchase cell packs of flowers or herbs and plant in small terra-cotta pots. Write one guest's name on each pot. Guests will know where to sit and have a nice gift to take home after the party.

Napkin rings: Tie a long sprig of rose-mary in a ring. As you bend the sprig of rosemary, gently break the stem so it gives a little when you bend it. You can add a dab of glue to keep the napkin rings in shape. But if you intertwine the rosemary, you shouldn't need the glue. You can also add accents by gluing a flower or a small pinecone to the napkin ring. Raffia works well for this. Tie the napkin with the raffia and slip fresh greens or blooms into the raffia.

Candle holders: Cut the top and center out of an artichoke, apple, melon, or any other fruit or vegetable. Insert a candle and voilà!

Place mats or plate chargers: Grab a cardboard pizza liner and glue leaves overlapping each other and the outer edges using floral adhesive. Pressed autumn leaves are spectacular, and so is fresh juniper. After you finish the outer edge, work from the outside toward the center and do the same thing on the inside portion of the cardboard, firmly pressing the leaves to the cardboard. Before you know it, you have a green, leafy place mat that will look stunning under your dishes. To finish it off with a burst of color, surround the dish with fresh baby carrots, pea pods, or beans.

Centerpiece: Fill baskets with a variety of vegetables. You can even tip a few baskets and arrange the vegetables so they appear to be pouring out.

Captivating champagne: If champagne is your beverage of choice for the event, make sure you have a platter of sweet herbs including scented geraniums. Have guests select and crush their herb of choice. Place it in the bottom of the champagne glass. Pour the champagne and enjoy the delicate fragrance from the herb.

Flowers Good Enough to Eat

FLOWER	EDIBLE PART
Borage	Flowers
Calendula	Petals
Chives	Stems and blossoms
Daylily	Flowers
Dianthus	Petals
Scented Geraniums	Leaves and petals
Hibiscus	Petals
Nasturtium	All parts
Viola	Flowers
Zucchini	Blossoms

When pruning your trees and shrubs, save the trimmings. They make excellent natural stakes. Insert the small twigs near the base of the plant and use the branches to cradle your flowers.

Extending the Life of Your Fresh Flowers

The big payoff from growing flowers is the bouquets you can enjoy both indoors and out. Gathering the bouquet is just a matter of snipping, but keeping it alive for a long time is the tricky part. With a few tips, you can stretch the life of these bouquets by a week.

Your first step is to find the freshest flowers available either from your backyard or the local grocery store. When you eyeball them, the flowers should be plump and just about ready to bloom. If they're drooping, don't pick them and don't buy them. In the store, look at the stems. They should be green and firm. If they're transparent or mushy, it's a sign they're headed for the compost pile.

Once you've picked the perfect bouquet, keep it in water as much as possible. Even when you get them home to arrange in a vase, cut them under water. If you don't, the sap in the stem will seal the waterway to the flowers. No water, no flower. Also, cut the stem at an angle, so the flower can draw up more water, eliminating stem clogging bacteria. As you arrange your flowers, remove leaves that are under water. They'll rot and contaminate the water. Once the flowers are arranged, change the water every couple of days, preferably with lukewarm water. The flower will draw up more that way. Also, mist the flowers to keep them fresh. Flower preservatives will make the flowers last, as will a splash of hydrogen peroxide.

Extending the life of your fresh cut flowers is as easy as reaching in your medicine cabinet. Adding a splash of hydrogen peroxide to the fresh water will kill the bacteria that destroy flowers.

Trees

They evoke stunning winter images of gnarly knots and winding wood. In the spring, a fragrant spray of flowers reaching for the sky covers the branches. By summer, they become striking canopies of green. Their season finale is a blazing display of color in the fall. Trees are the backbone of the landscape around us. Most people think of trees for shade and maybe fall color. But there is more to a tree than meets the eye.

Trees are a vital source of life around us. In the heat of summer trees provide a protective canopy of foliage that helps give relief from the sun. In the winter, a tree placed 100 feet to the north and west of your home will shield it from those wicked winter winds. It can even cut your heating bills by as much as 20 percent. Trees can be used as a sound barrier between busy streets and your home. They also help filter pollution from automobile exhaust. Trees added to any landscape also add value to the home.

BASIC NEEDS

The first rule of thumb is: Trees are not furniture. I see it so often. People notice a beautiful tree growing in someone's yard. They buy and plant the same variety in their yard only to watch it slowly die. Trees are not like furniture. Just because they look good in a yard across town doesn't mean they'll look as good in your yard. So before you head to the store here are the questions you should be asking yourself:

What kind of soil do you have? Some trees are quite finicky about the soil in which they grow. If you have clay soil, don't expect a tree that needs loose, well-drained soil to thrive in your yard.

How much sun will the tree get? Full sun means direct sun can be expected 8 to 10 hours every day. An area considered partial shade gets only 6 hours of sun. And deep shade means just that: Sun is filtered through trees or blocked by buildings for most of the day.

How tall do you want the tree to get? The tree may be small to start with, but it will grow taller than you might think. And it will spread as well. You need to know your space limitations. How close will it be to the house or the garage next door?

What are your expectations? Do you want vivid fall color, flowers, fruit, arching branches, or an upright conical shape? You need answers to these very important questions to satisfy your expectations. And you should be specific with your plans, because there are different types of trees to fit everyone's needs.

Once you've answered the above questions, take your ideas to your neighborhood garden center.

BUYING TREES

Now that you've armed yourself with sufficient information, it's time to pick the perfect tree. As you'll see, trees come in all shapes and sizes. Typically the bigger the tree, the bigger the price you'll pay. Yet, smaller trees are easier to establish in the home landscape and obviously easier to plant.

Once you've picked out a tree, examine it carefully. The trunk should stand upright or straight. Stay away from any that have a tendency to lean or have any weird kinks in the trunk. Also make sure there are no deep scars or nicks in the bark. Minor scrapes are normal, deep ones are not. The branches should be evenly balanced around the tree. Any foliage should be a rich green color. Leaves with a ragged appearance indicate insect damage.

Trees are sold either bare-root, in containers, or balled-and-burlapped. The least expensive are bare-root trees, which are available only in spring. These are trees whose roots are exposed, not buried in soil.

Typically roots are covered in moist peat moss. Bare-root trees are an excellent way of getting a very healthy tree at a huge price reduction. The only catch is that bare-root trees must be planted right away before leaves emerge and the roots must remain moist at all times. Once the tree is at home it's a good practice to sink the roots into a large bucket of water for at least three hours. When planting the tree you must be very careful to keep moist peat moss around the roots until the tree is actually planted.

The most common way to buy trees is in containers. You can buy some time with these, as they don't require immediate planting. Just be sure to water as needed until you're ready to plant and remove the containers completely before you plant.

And finally there are balled-and-burlapped trees. These are more expensive. What makes these trees a good choice is that the tree is taken directly from the fields without much disturbance to the root ball and wrapped in burlap. The root ball is larger than those of most containerized trees, which is healthier for the tree. If planting a balled-and-burlapped ("b-and-b") tree, remove any synthetic material that won't decompose. Many b-and-b trees have wire cages. I personally try to avoid these if I can. Although the wire is supposed to rust away, it takes too long for my liking. I've seen dead trees pulled from holes with the wire cage still intact. The burlap around the root ball can be left on only if it will rot away. If it stretches when you pull it, it probably contains plastic and will suffocate the roots. When placing a b-and-b tree, be careful to pick it up by the root ball and not the trunk and be extra careful to keep the root ball intact.

PLANTING

The timing of planting can be critical to some trees. The general rule is that summer planting should be avoided in all locations. Spring planting is best for climates in zone 4 and lower. For zones 5 to 7 (see "Know Your Zone" on p. xvi), spring is still the best time to plant, although trees planted in the fall usually have enough time to establish themselves before winter sets in. In the warmer climates where there's hardly a winter, trees will do better if planted in the fall or winter because spring temperatures can warm up too quickly and stress the tree.

Before you even begin to dig, you must know where your underground utility cables or wires are buried. Allow one to two weeks to have your yard marked by utility companies. Make sure you avoid digging in marked areas. Now it's time to get your hands dirty. The techniques of planting trees have changed through the years. However one standard practice of planting trees has withstood the test of time.

The first thing you must do is measure the width of the root ball. This will clue you in as to how wide to dig your hole for planting. The hole should be at least 1½ times as wide as the root ball and the depth should be equal to the depth of the tree in the container. When figuring how deep to make the hole, remember that the depth is critical. More often than not trees are troubled as a result of being buried too deeply.

At the base of every tree is a swollen area. On grafted trees it is more pronounced and looks like a knob. This is called the bud union. The knobby joint is much less obvious on trees that are not grafted. The swollen area is referred to as a root flare. Both the bud union and the root flare are great barometers for the planting depth of trees. These joints should be above the soil (about 1 inch above) and never below.

Remove the soil and set it aside. Years ago it was advised to enrich the soil with manure, etc. However studies show that the trees are actually better off establishing themselves in surrounding soil. If you overamend the soil, the roots have no reason to stretch their "legs" in search for nutrients—it's all right there. But it's important for roots to spread to anchor the tree.

If, however, your soil is heavy clay, very sandy, or not very fertile, you should add some amendments. But don't overdo it. Compost or rotted manure are the best choices for amending. Peat moss is fine if used in very small doses.

Once the hole is dug, deeply score the side of the hole with a garden fork or sharp shovel. This helps minimize any glazing that may have occurred as you dug the hole. (Friction from the shovel blade rubbing against the soil smears soil particles together, making it tough for young roots to penetrate.) Now you're ready to plant the tree.

If the tree is in a container, wire cage, or synthetic burlap, gently remove it. Place the tree in the hole. Lay the handle of the shovel or a board across the hole. Where's the bud union? It should be above the board or handle. If not, carefully remove the tree, add more soil

Spring

to the bottom of the hole. Firm the soil to prevent settling and try the tree again. Where's the root flare? It should be just below the board or handle.

Planting can be a little more tricky with bare-root trees. Remember while digging and testing the depth, never let the roots sit without water or wet peat moss around them. If the roots dry, the tree dies. Getting the right calculations for the hole's depth is the hardest part, since there is no solid root ball. Once the hole seems appropriate, have one person gently place the tree in the soil and hold it steady while the other person spreads the roots and makes sure the depth is appropriate. Gradually add the soil while the person holding the tree gently toggles the tree up and down. This will help the soil settle in around the roots.

For any kind of tree, once the hole is halfway full, add water. This will help remove any large air pockets. Continue backfilling once the water has drained. Firm the soil at the base of the tree with your hands, making a well around the tree as you go. This saucer will trap water and trickle it down to the tree's root system. Be generous with the saucer. Think of the size of the root ball—will the water get there from your saucer?

STAKING

Not all trees need to be staked. But giving your new tree support is important if the site is exposed to strong winds. The purpose of staking is to help anchor the roots. However, don't overdo it because the tree needs to bend a little with the wind to toughen the trunk.

Here's a technique I've used that works like a charm on younger trees. Try using a vinyl ribbon called "stretch-tie" used for tying vines to a trellis. Most garden centers sell it. Wrap the ribbon around the tree and attach it to a hard plastic tent stake pounded 4 to 6 inches into the ground. Since the vinyl stretches, it doesn't girdle the trunk and allows the tree to move as the wind blows while

keeping the roots in place. Place one stake in the face of the prevailing wind; others should be equally spaced around the tree. Usually three or four do the trick. In time the wind will cause the vinyl to stretch and loosen. Simply wind any excess around the tent stakes. Typically after one year, the roots should be anchored well enough that you can remove the stakes.

Another more traditional method is done with 3- to 5-foot-tall grape stakes, which are driven into the ground about 2 to 4 inches deep and 6 to 12 inches away from the root ball of the tree. Twine is tied onto the stakes and then wrapped around the trunk. Since the twine will cut into the bark if direct contact is made, run it through a short length of old garden hose wrapped around the tree. And again remember that the supports should not be too tight.

WATERING AND FEEDING

Hopefully there will be enough rainfall to keep your tree watered. Trees need about an inch a week. What's an inch? You can put a tuna can under the tree to measure. And what about fertilizer? Opinions differ, but typically newly planted trees don't need fertilizer. As the tree is growing you may want to feed it, but be sure to stop fertilizing eight weeks before the first frost. You don't want to encourage new growth when the tree needs to start preparing for winter.

Tree Pruning Pointers

Knowing when and how to prune can be confusing. Here are some general guidelines:

- *Hardwood trees without flowers: best pruned in winter or early spring.*
- *Conifers: may be pruned any time of the year.*
- *Flowering trees: if they flower in early spring, prune immediately after flowering. (Pruning later cuts off the buds of next year's flowers.) If they bloom later, prune when dormant.*
- *Dead branches can be removed anytime.*
- *Trees that bleed sap should be pruned in late spring or summer.*

COMMON TREE PROBLEMS

Trees aren't without their troubles. Many get sick and need help to survive. You might encounter the following common problems:

Black Knot

If your tree has black, ragged, swollen or elongated sections on the limbs it probably is suffering from a disease called black knot, which is caused by a fungus.

The fungus enters the tree's tender tissue in the spring. Within two years the affected area will develop a black, elongated, woody swollen area (gall) on the stem. This fungus affects cherries, chokecherries, and any trees that produce fruit with a large pit.

Cure: In early spring, before the leaves appear, examine the tree's stems for swollen areas. These indicate infection from last year. Measure about 4 to 5 inches back from the base of the swollen area and cut off the branch at this point to remove the infection. Also prune out areas with the bigger black galls that are obvious. Black knot will not kill the tree, it's just not very attractive.

Shoot Blight

If the needles on your pine tree are turning brown, there are a number of different diseases that might be affecting it. But one very common disease is called "shoot blight." It infects the new shoots of two- and three-needle pines. The infection starts in the spring just as the new shoots start growing. It will kill the needles, leaving a dead area on the tip of the branch.

You can tell if your pine has shoot blight by looking at the ends of the branches. New growth should be soft and green. If it's brown you probably have shoot blight. Cut a sample and take it to a garden center or county extension service for diagnosis and treatment recommendations.

Cure: If the diagnosis is shoot blight, cut out the infected shoots. The following spring, apply a fungicide to protect the new growth when it emerges. Ask your garden center or Cooperative Extension Service which fungicides will be effective for this disease, as not all fungicides will work.

Cankers

Cankers are a common problem on trees, especially maples. You've seen them before: big round knots in the trunk. Cankers are usually caused by some type of a wound, such as a nick by the lawn mower or improper pruning, and sometimes from winter weather. A fungus enters the wound and over a number of years causes the canker.

Cure: Cankers won't kill the tree, but they can weaken it. Once you spy damage, keep the tree as healthy as possible with mulching and water and minimal fertilizer. But if the canker continues to spread and grow in size, the tree should be removed. Cankers can weaken the tree's trunk so much that it falls over, which can be hazardous, if not deadly.

BLOOMING TREES

Among the first signs of spring are the beautiful blooms on flowering trees. Not only do they look great, many smell terrific. Too bad the blooms last for just a couple of weeks. There are many varieties of blooming trees. Some of the most popular are ornamental forms of fruit trees.

The rules for planting blooming trees are the same as for regular trees. Again, remember spring is the best time to plant since the roots will have a good opportunity to establish themselves before it gets too hot. Early fall is the second choice.

Six Blooming Trees to Get You Started

Juneberry or Serviceberry: These trees get high marks for their drooping clusters of snowy white or pinkish flowers that bloom in early spring. Enjoy the blooms while you can because they last only a short time.

Flowering Plums: Plums are excellent for the home landscape. The trees offer an abundance of fragrant blooms with terrific beauty and color. After the blossoms drop, many trees produce small yellow, red, blue, or purple fruit while the "hybrid" plum forms no fruit at all (a good choice for those who just want the spring show). Most plum trees grow to a height of 10 to 20 feet tall. Plums don't like standing in water so make sure soil is well-drained. They like full sun but are affected by winter winds. Prune after the tree blooms.

Mountain Ash: A very hardy tree, mountain ash has fernlike foliage and white, flat-topped flowers in the spring. Its small, berrylike fruits attract birds but can be messy when they fall to the ground. Also look for Korean Mountain Ash and European Mountain Ash, but be aware that both are susceptible to fire blight. The disease spreads by pruning, so ask your nursery when to prune your specific tree. It's important to realize that fire blight is a bacterial disease and therefore can't be controlled with fungicide.

Magnolias: Long considered a symbol of the South, there are magnolia hybrids that grow well in northern climates, too. Their showy spring flowers and succulent leaves are their trademark. With magnolias, one must be patient, as some of the trees take up to three years to bloom. Star Magnolia grows to 6 to 10 feet and Umbrella Magnolia can grow up to 40 feet tall with larger leaves.

Catalpa: Catalpa trees grow delicate flowers that look like orchids. When the flowers fade, heart-shaped leaves bud, and long green bean-shaped seed capsules take center stage.

Crabapples and Apples: Their spectacular spring bouquets make flowering crabapples and apple trees a mainstay of the spring landscape. Crabapples bloom in a variety of colors; apple blooms change from pink to white. For both kinds of trees, plant two different varieties within 1,000 feet of each other so they can pollinate each other and bear fruit. Hardy varieties of crabapples are 'Candied Apple,' 'Kelsey,' 'Prairifire,' or 'Spring Snow.' Good apple varieties for northern climates are 'Honeygold,' 'Honey Crisp,' and 'Haralred.'

Shrubs

Today, families are busier than ever, so looking for shortcuts is a matter of survival or at least the means to keeping sane. And in the garden, shortcuts are a must for many. But just because you can't devote a lot of time to planting and pruning doesn't mean you can't have a fabulous landscape—you just have to be a little more selective in what you plant. And that's where shrubs come in. Not only do they mature quickly, they're easy to maintain. They don't want much from you except a good location, decent soil, and food and drink when necessary. With proper care,

they'll probably outlive your stay in the home.

Before you head out to the garden center it's very important for you to do a little homework. You must decide what the purpose of the shrubs will be. Are they merely to block the view to the neighbor's yard? Or are you expecting to create a certain feel or look with them? Once you've decided on their purpose, it's worth scanning books and catalogues to see some of the choices you have. As you'll see, shrubs come in all shapes, sizes, textures, and colors. Some bloom, others don't. Some are evergreen (retain their greenery all year), while others are deciduous (drop their leaves in the fall). Some have spectacular bark. Some creep along the ground while others tower into the sky. The selections are nearly endless. And keep in mind that garden centers don't carry all the shrubs that are available. Some may have to be bought through mail-order catalogues. Once you've got a good feel for what you're looking for, it's time to shop.

BUYING

As you shop for shrubs, remember the golden garden rule: If the plant doesn't look good and healthy, it probably isn't. So don't waste your money. Here's what a healthy plant should look like: It should be balanced, with equal lengths of foliage around the entire plant. Stay away from anything that has brown leaves. Examine the plant care-fully, looking for insects or insect damage; many of the insects will hide on the undersides of the foliage so be sure to check there and look closely. Some of these critters can hardly be seen with the naked eye. Another clue to a healthy plant is one without any deep nicks or scars in the bark. And finally check the main stalk or stem. It should stand upright without any wild kinks (which might lead to a less than spectacular sight) unless of course it's supposed to be weeping or twisted.

The next decision you'll have to make is whether to buy the shrubs wrapped in burlap or in plastic pots. The burlap will cost you a little more, but it might be worth it because the plant hasn't been transplanted and will have a larger root ball.

Now what size container should you start with? That all depends on your pocketbook. The smaller the plant, the

Six Super Shrubs for Starters

SHRUB	ZONES	HEIGHT
Dwarf Boxwood	5	2–3 ft.
Red Cedar	2	1½–40 ft.
Alpine Currant	2	4–7 ft.
Siberian Dogwood	2–8	8–10 ft.
Juniper	2	½–20 ft.
Potentilla	2	4 in.–3 ft.

Shrubs

less money you'll have to put out. However, here's something to consider. Initially it's going to take about a year and a half to get a plant in a 3-gallon container to grow to the size of one in a 5-gallon container. And the plant in the 1-gallon container will take a year and a half to grow to the size of the plant in the 3-gallon container. So if you can't wait for bigger results and have the cash, then go for the larger plant.

> *No matter what size containerized shrub you buy, within three to four years they'll all be the same size.*

PLANTING

Shrubs aren't too picky about soil, but they always prefer well-drained, loamy soil, which makes their roots spread much more easily. Be sure the plant receives adequate light. The requirements differ with each shrub; check the plant tag or ask the garden center for details.

Before you start digging, calculate how big the plant will get when it matures and then determine where the plant will go. Too often people crowd shrubs together because they look good clustered when they're small. But once they start growing they'll need to be pulled out because they're either too close to each other or too close to the house. Dig a hole that's twice as wide as

the container and just about as deep. If the soil is good, then don't amend. If you have sandy or clay soil you may want to add some peat moss, compost, and rotted manure to improve the consistency.

Gently remove the plant from its container and examine the roots. They should be creamy white. If you see broken or brown, soggy roots, remove them with pruning shears. And if the roots have wound themselves around the base of the bucket, untangle them or loosen them by making slits around the base. This helps loosen the roots and allows them to get established more quickly.

Gently place the plant in the hole. The plant should stand slightly higher in the hole than it was in its container. Backfill half the soil then water thoroughly. This will not only give the plant a good drink but will also allow excess air bubbles to escape. Then finish filling. You should make a small saucer around the newly planted shrub to help catch

Spring

- *If the shrub blooms in the spring, prune in the fall.*

- *If it blooms in the summer and fall, prune in winter or early spring before leaves appear.*

- *Evergreen pruning is best done when the shrub is actively growing. Besides keeping the shrub in check, pruning is done to remove dead, diseased, or damaged limbs. But you should verify with the variety.*

water for the plant. To finish it off add a generous layer of mulch. Three to five inches of mulch will prevent weeds from growing, but the mulch also helps retain water, cools the soil, and looks nice. There are a variety of mulches to choose from and the choice is really up to you. Just remember the chunkier the mulch, the slower it decomposes.

PRUNING SHRUBS

Before you pick up those pruning shears, make sure you know when the plant is supposed to be pruned. Many shrubs set flowers on new and old wood. That's important to know because untimely pruning will chop off next season's blossoms. Since every shrub is different, I suggest you investigate each shrub's needs and keep a journal to remind you what needs to be pruned and when.

LIVING FENCES

When most people build a fence it's usually made with wood or wire.

Some can be beautiful, while others are unnatural eyesores. A great option is a living fence, trees or shrubs that, over time, will give you privacy and a living green wall.

Many trees and shrubs make excellent hedges and if planted correctly can literally outlive the wood or wire fences. Before heading to the garden center make a checklist to help with your plant selection.

- *Do you want greenery all winter long?*

- *How much can you afford to spend?*

- *What kind of sun will the plants receive?*

- *How tall do you want your hedge to grow?*

- *Do you want a formal (pruned) or informal (unpruned) look?*

Let's start with greenery. Evergreens are great choices for living fences. These are plants that keep their leaves all winter long. One very popular choice is arborvitae. Different varieties of arborvitae grow from 2 to 20 feet. They like sun to part shade and can be pruned for a formal look. They will cost more money than the deciduous plants.

Deciduous plants are another choice. These are plants that lose their leaves during the winter months. They don't cost as much but like the evergreens mature to varying heights. Since there are so many varieties of deciduous trees and shrubs, finding one to fit your specific criteria shouldn't be a problem. Some recommendations: Chinese lilac, viburnum, and alpine currant.

The key to creating a good hedge or living fence comes in the tight spacing of the plants. The rule for most plants is about 1 to 3 feet apart. Spacing farther apart ensures better health but you'll have to wait longer for the plants to close in.

Lawns

The love for lawns goes back thousands of years. The Chinese grew grass over 5,000 years ago. In thirteenth-century Europe, manicured lawns were considered a status symbol. It was only the most wealthy Europeans who were able to surround their property with a lush green carpet. Today people still surround themselves with lush, green lawns but for different reasons.

We sit on it. Roll on it. And run and play on it. We put it in, we cut it. Grass is the common thread of most homeowners. Whether it's just a strip or mammoth acreage, Americans are fanatical about their lawns. Achieving that terrific turf means starting off on the right foot—from the ground up.

SOIL PREPARATION

A lush green lawn requires healthy, rich soil. You must enrich your soil before you plant your new turf. If you must have soil delivered, consider this: The topsoil may look dark and fertile, but there's no guarantee that the pile of soil you paid for is rich in nutrients. More often than not the soil dumped in your yard was the soil from the basement that was just dug up from the new house down the road. There are no regulations for topsoil. Someone is making a lot of money at your expense! If you really want a lush, green, healthy lawn, you have to enrich the soil. Enriching doesn't mean just a topdressing of compost, manure, or peat moss. It means mixing these ingredients in with the soil, just like preparing a garden bed. Spread a thick, generous layer of compost, manure, and peat moss. Then sprinkle fertilizer over the top. With a rototiller mix it in to a depth of at least 6 inches. This will help bring up large debris like rocks, sticks, or leftover bricks the builder was too lazy to remove. Clean out the debris and rake the surface smooth. You might want to burn some rubber over the new bed—that means dragging a rubber tire across the soil. This helps smooth, level, and remove small debris. Then water the soil. This helps it settle. Once the soil has dried somewhat, it's a good idea to run the tiller over the area again. Let the area settle for a week before planting.

TECHNIQUES

Establishing a lawn is not very difficult, depending on which technique you choose. There are basically three ways of growing a lawn: seeding, hydro-seeding, or planting sod. Seeding is the least expensive but most labor intensive. It will take about seven days for the seeds to germinate and about three weeks before the ground is covered with green. Hydro-seeding is done commercially. A big truck loaded with a wet pulp of shredded newspapers mixed with grass seed and fertilizer squirts a glue-like substance over your property. Within weeks the soil is covered with new blades of grass. The third method is sod—the most expensive of the three—but immediate. You'll have grass by the afternoon.

The best time to install a lawn is the cool spring and fall weather.

SEEDING

If you're lean on cash but need a lawn, seeding will help your budget. It does require more work and attention from you, but in the long run you'll have beautiful, long lasting healthy turf.

The key to a healthy lawn comes from good, viable seeds that will do well in your area. I recommend going to a reputable garden center and buying in bulk. The reasons are simple. You'll save money, plus the bulk seeds are usually mixed by the garden center or someone locally, which means the combination is guaranteed to do well in your climate. If you buy seeds by the box, plan on spending more money for packaging and be sure to check the date for freshness. The important thing is to buy seeds exactly mixed for your climate and sun requirements. There should be no more than four different varieties mixed together. More than that and your lawn will look blotchy. Also, the "inert material" (by-products of harvesting) should be no more than 2 percent of the total. You also should consider what the lawn will be used for. If the kids are going to be playing football, you'll need a tougher turf. There are seeds that will fit your needs.

STEP-BY-STEP:
SEEDING

- *Fill a drop spreader or a whirly-bird with seed.*

- *Start walking. The seed will fly, and the goal is to make sure it's evenly spread.*

- *For the tight areas that the whirly-bird can't reach, just do it manually.*

- *Once the seeds are down, you have to keep them down—otherwise they*

will wash away with the first rain. That's where mulch comes in. Mulching anchors grass seeds while retaining moisture. Straw has been used for years; however, it can be quite messy and will fly when the first gust of wind blows. I prefer to spread a thin layer of peat moss. It can absorb a lot of moisture and stays in one place. The drenched peat takes on a darker tone and that works to your advantage. As it dries, the color transforms into a lighter hue. When the peat becomes lighter, it's nature's way of telling you your new seedbed is ready for more water.

- *It's critical to keep the seeds well watered during the first week to ten days. In hot, dry weather that may mean watering your new lawn morning, noon, and night.*

When you're done, the seed should look like this:

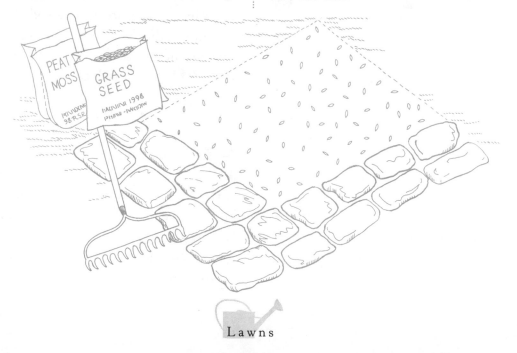

Hydro-Seeding

Hydro-seeding is my preferred choice for establishing a new lawn. It must be done professionally, and it will cost more than seeding.

Hydro-seeding combines all the crucial elements of seeding: the seeds, shredded phone books or newspapers for mulch, and fertilizer. This is all mixed together and then soaked with water just prior to application. It is sprayed out as a sticky, glue-like substance. This keeps the seed from washing away and is particularly effective on sloped areas. As with seeding, it is important to keep the new seeds watered during the first seven to ten days.

> *Stay off new turf until the new lawn is up and growing and has been mowed at least twice.*

Laying Sod

For those of you who want instant gratification, sod is definitely the way to go. But have your wallet handy. It will cost more than any other technique. You can reduce the amount you spend if you lay the sod yourself, but be prepared—it will take a full afternoon to finish anywhere from a quarter to a third of an acre.

After the soil is prepared, it's important to remove about 1 inch of soil along the edge of the sidewalk or driveway. Sod sheets are about an inch thick and you don't want them sticking up higher than the pavement. Now you're ready to roll out the green carpet! It's best to start from the outside and work in. That will ensure nice clean edges. Push the sod pieces right up to the edge. The tighter the fit, the fewer seams you'll see. As you lay the next piece, think of a brick pattern. You don't want all the seams lining up. If you stagger sod strips, all the seams are mismatched and hard to find. Staggering also helps to disperse water. As you lay each piece side by side, again try to make a very tight fit. As soon as you're done rolling out all the sod, water it thoroughly. That will help settle the sod into the soil. Water in the morning and again in the afternoon. The sod should stay moist the first couple of weeks to give the new roots a chance to spread and establish themselves.

MOWING

Never mow off more than one-third of the grass height. In southern climates, cut grass to 2 inches high, and in northern climates, to 3 inches high. Longer grass helps promote deeper, more drought-tolerant roots, helps smother weeds, and keeps the soil cool

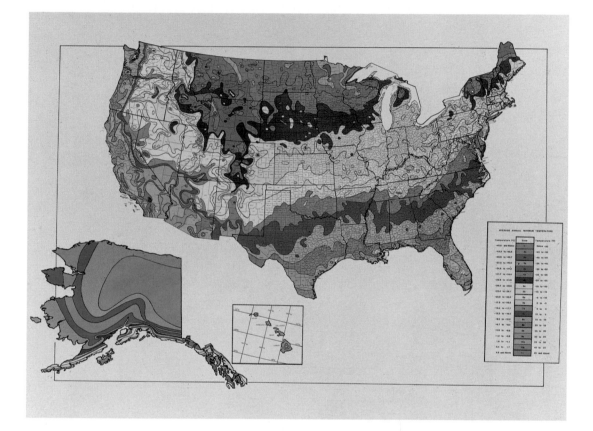

▲ Knowing your zone
Courtesy of the Agricultural Research Service, USDA

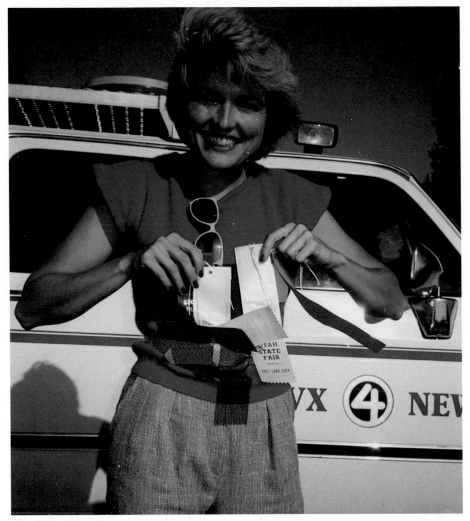

▲ How it all began

▲ Digging for black gold

◀ Rebecca getting approval
from her mentor
*Photos by Doug Beasley, courtesy
of* Rebecca's Garden Magazine

▲ A burst of spring color

Photo by Andrew Kessler, courtesy of Hearst-Argyle Television Productions

while also retaining more moisture. When you mow, leave the clippings on the lawn. They will break down quickly and provide a small shot of nitrogen. If you leave them on after every mowing, research indicates that you can reduce the need for fertilizer by 25 percent.

WATERING

Newly planted grass needs plenty of water for the first two weeks to ensure seed germination. Established grass needs water on a regular basis. Each watering should soak down into the root zone about 6 to 8 inches. Each climate is different, but typically during the hottest period of the summer most lawns will need about 2 inches of water a week. You'll know your lawn needs a drink if the grass stays matted down after you walk on it.

FEEDING

Lawns are heavy feeders of nitrogen—and too much is not better! Each bag of fertilizer is different, but all will have three numbers listed on the front. The first number is the percentage of nitrogen. This is important for lawns. Selecting a bag with a high number is good since nitrogen is one of the most important elements in developing a thick, attractive lawn. Three applications can be made on the lawn during the growing season. The first application should come in spring, the second in early summer, and the last in late fall. Never fertilize during the hottest part of the summer.

Applying Fertilizer

The best way to apply fertilizer is with a drop spreader. If you don't have one, many garden centers or hardware centers will rent you one. Calibrate the setting of the drop spreader before you pour the fertilizer into the bin. Instructions on the bag of fertilizer will tell you which setting to use. However, if you want to get excellent coverage without leaving stripes on your lawn, do what I do. If the directions tell you to set your spreader on 6, divide in half and set the spreader on 3. Apply half your fertilizer walking in one direction across the lawn. Apply the remaining half of your fertilizer in a direction perpendicular to your first pass across the lawn.

PATCHING DEAD SPOTS

Our lawns take a beating. Regardless of how hard we try, kids, dogs, lawn mowers, or varmints create a dead spot or two. Not to worry—dead spots are easy to repair, especially with some of the new products available today.

The most inexpensive way to patch dead spots is with seeds. All you need to do is scrape out all the dead grass. (Set it aside; use it for mulch.) Then score the soil surface. Scratch in some fertilizer. Spread the grass seed over the top, using your hands to keep it in place. Cover lightly with dead grass clippings or peat moss. Water well without washing the seed away. Keep moist until the seed germinates. In about five to seven days you'll see new blades of grass sprouting.

You can now buy a bag that has everything you need for patching: seeds, mulch, and fertilizer. You still have to clean out the dead debris and score the soil. Then add a handful of the concoction and spread it out evenly. Water and keep moist until the grass appears. The mulch mats down, holding your seed in place, and eventually decomposes. This product works especially well on sloped areas.

WEED CONTROL

A lawn with no weeds is one that has probably been chemically treated. However, good, thick grass will smother most weeds. I don't spray mine and granted, it may not be as weed free as the neighbor's, but I have pets and children and prefer not to take risks with any sort of pesticide, herbicide, or anything toxic. Plus it's not the natural way.

Dogs love lawns as much as we do. But what they leave behind can kill the grass—or burn it. Here's a trick my mom told me. Feed your dog 2 tablespoons of tomato juice every day. Supposedly it neutralizes the dog's urine so it's not so acidic. People who've tried this trick swear by it.

Gardening is "dirty" work—literally! To wash away the evidence, insert a small bar of soap into the end of a nylon stocking. Tie the stocking around an outdoor spigot. When finished gardening, you can clean up outside before going inside.

Fertilizer 101

Are you confused by the numbers on bags of fertilizer? You're not alone—so are many gardeners. What makes it so difficult is that there are so many different bags with different combinations of numbers. How do you know which one you need?

The three numbers look something like this: 20-10-15. The first number represents nitrogen, the second phosphorus, and the third potassium. Each number represents the amount of that particular nutrient in the bag. For instance, the "20" means that 20 percent

Spring

of the contents in the bag are nitrogen, a nutrient necessary for lush green leaf growth. Grass does especially well with a good dose of nitrogen, particularly in the spring. The second number means the bag contains 10 percent phosphate (a form of phosphorus). Phosphorus is essential for healthy fruiting crops and flowers. And the third number tells the percentage of potash (the common form of potassium). Potassium builds good roots and a strong immune system for the plant. What you're growing will dictate which combinations of numbers you should get. The remaining percentage is filler, material that helps the product spread easily.

If you're still confused, an all-purpose general fertilizer 10-10-10 is good for all lawns and gardens. Whatever you use, don't overdo it. Too much fertilizer will damage the plants. Read the label and follow recommended application rates. When in doubt, cut back.

Fertilizer Facts

Organic fertilizers: Nutrients from dead plant material. No synthetic additives.

Slow-release fertilizers: Products that are impregnated with fertilizers. The outer shell of the products slowly breaks down as it interacts with moisture and soil, releasing fertilizer as it goes. Some last three to nine months.

Granular fertilizers: Most common. Grains containing fertilizer will dissolve when moistened.

Liquid fertilizers: Concentrated fertilizer that must be diluted with water before applying. More expensive.

Lawns

Spring
Projects

GARDENS IN POTS

The nice thing about gardening is that you don't need acreage or even a backyard to grow some of the most popular flowers and vegetables. All you really need is a pot and sunshine. Picking the perfect pot is very important. If the pot is too small, plants will need watering every day. Full sun and heat can be deadly elements for plants trying to thrive in pots. For such cases light-colored plastic pots may be the perfect choice for you. They don't dry out as quickly as the terra-cotta pots do. Your plant will stay moist longer.

Terra-cotta (clay) pots, on the other hand, are porous; they let water evaporate. That means you'll have to water more often. Clay pots are great for shady locations.

The soil going into your pots should be mixtures high in compost or peat moss. These keep soil light and airy so it doesn't suffocate the plant roots like heavier soils. Before adding the plants, you may want to mix in a slow-release fertilizer. Otherwise, you'll have to fertilize the plants every two weeks. Excessive watering washes away nutrients quickly.

When selecting plants to go into the pots, combine those that have the same watering needs. Geraniums work well with petunias, impatiens with pansies. And don't skimp on the number of plants per pot. Pack 'em in! The most dramatic pots are those overflowing with waves of color and texture.

No More Heavy Pots!

No need to break your back trying to move a large pot of petunias. Most annual flowers need only about 10 inches of soil to thrive. So why waste so much soil that just weighs you down? Here's a tip to lighten your load. Fill the bottom of a large pot with plastic packing peanuts, inverted plastic pots, aluminum cans, or plastic milk jugs. Cover the top of the "filler" with landscape fabric. This allows the water to drain but will keep the soil in place. Add soil and plant as usual. You've just reduced the weight of your pot.

ATTRACTING BUTTERFLIES

A big part of your gardening experience is attracting wildlife by growing the right combination of flowers and plants. Birds, bees, butterflies, and hummingbirds enjoy beautiful flowers as much as we do. To attract them, all you have to do is find out what each species likes to munch on for a snack. If it's but-terflies you want, you have to work fast. Our colorful fluttering friends live about two weeks, on average. They will come if you grow flowers for nectar and host plants for breeding. You must combine the two types of plants if you want the butterflies to come. But it's more than just that. The location of your butterfly garden is important, too. Butterflies need sun and lots of it to keep warm.

Butterflies will flock to your garden if you provide lots of nectar plants. Two of the most common are zinnias and Mexican sunflowers. These will grow anywhere in the country. Other nectar plants include: aster, butterfly bush, butterfly weed, black-eyed Susan, coreopsis (tickseed), Joe-Pye weed, lantana, and purple coneflowers.

However, nectar plants alone are not enough. Host plants serve as a breeding ground and feed hungry caterpillars. Host plants might already be growing in your backyard. They include milkweed, parsley, and dill. Other host plants include: aster, cabbage, broccoli, lupine, Queen-Anne's-lace, snapdragons, violets, vetch, and sedum.

Pesticides thwart any hope of attracting these winged beauties. Don't even think about using pesticides if you want butterflies to punctuate your garden's natural beauty.

ATTRACTING HUMMINGBIRDS

Hummingbirds move very quickly but are easy to attract. They like flowers, especially those that are red and tubular, but will come to a feeder too. Like the butterflies, hummingbirds will come if you have the right ingredient— lots of flowers. Select flowers that have different blooming schedules so the tiny birds will visit all summer long. Since red tubular flowers tend to have more nectar, hummingbirds are attracted to them but will visit other flowers too. Two of the most popular are red salvia and trumpet creeper vine. Other hummingbird attractions include: bleeding-heart, delphinium, lilies, mint, morning glory, phlox, snapdragon, trumpet honeysuckle, and sweet William.

Feeders

Hang a couple of hummingbird feeders loaded with sweet nectar. It's a natural cocktail even the busiest hummingbird will find time to enjoy! Hummingbird feeders can be purchased at any bird store or hardware store or at some garden centers. If you hang one, you must commit to keeping it full of food and to keeping it clean. Once the hummingbirds visit your yard they'll return year after year as long as there is food.

Hang the feeder just prior to the bird's arrival. (Check with your local bird store for the specific date.) To get the most business at your feeder locate it near flowers, out of direct sunlight, and away from windy areas. Fill the feeder with sugar water. The water must be changed every couple of days or it will ferment and turn sour. Clean your feeder in hot water at the same time.

> *It's easy to make your own hummingbird food. Mix 1 part sugar with 4 parts distilled water. Boil for 1 to 2 minutes. Cool and store extra in refrigerator.*

> *Hummingbirds know when to migrate. Let them tell you when it's time. When they quit showing up you can take the feeder down. In other words, they won't stick around just because your feeder is up!*

Spring

Spring Garden

Checklist

- *Repair or replace broken or worn-out gardening gear.*
- *Sharpen lawn mower blades.*
- *Sharpen pruning shears.*
- *Figure out date of last expected frost.*
- *As temperatures warm, slowly pull back winter mulch from perennials and roses.*
- *Prune roses.*
- *Let the soil dry out before digging.*
- *Prune trees before bud break. Also, many shrubs can be pruned—but not those that flower in the spring.*
- *Test soil.*
- *Move transplants outdoors. Start by leaving plants in shade. Over two-week period gradually move plants to sunny location.*
- *Start a new lawn and patch dead spots before temperature gets too warm.*
- *Prevent powdery mildew on plants and flowers by spraying now.*
- *Control crabgrass early in the season.*
- *Fertilize lawns after three mowings.*
- *Don't bag lawn clippings; leave them on the lawn.*
- *Aerate lawn to improve soil and grass growth.*
- *Unwrap winter protection from trees and shrubs.*
- *Let foliage from bulbs die back naturally. Fertilize when foliage turns from green to yellow.*
- *Plant warm-season crops after danger of frost has passed.*
- *Introduce a new vegetable or flower to your garden.*
- *Stake tomatoes and taller flowers before they reach full height.*

Summer

. . . the growing season

Summer is the time gardens come alive. The infusion of warm sunshine kicks plants into high gear. Garden colors are vivid and vegetables are nearing harvest. Summer is also the tough season. Most gardeners start to run out of steam. All the energy and enthusiasm they had in the last few months has been exhausted. But now more than ever it's very important to stay on top of the garden.

Competition in the garden is high. As a gardener, you must constantly be on the lookout. There are crawling critters in search of a tasty morsel. They can destroy plants in days. However, the biggest offender in your garden is not a winged or crawling insect but weeds! They can invade the garden almost overnight. They choke plants, rob them of nutrients and water, and grow with a vigor unmatched by anything else. And what's worse, we can tug and pull but they keep coming back!

Vegetable

Follow-up

The vegetable garden should be cranking now. Keep an eye on your cucumbers and zucchini. If they look ripe and ready (typically 6 to 8 inches long), go for it! If you don't pick them, they'll turn into mammoth monsters overnight! If that happens the plant will slow down production of future vegetables.

Workwise, summer gardening is a cinch; it's the weather you have to worry about. Too much rain creates a fungus fest. Drought can suck the life out of a plant in days. And severe summer storms can rip up a garden. Many of the evil episodes can't be helped, but others can.

WEEDING

Weeds will steal nutrients and water from your plants. And now, more than any other time of the growing season, the plants don't need competition. It's important to keep out the weeds. Pulling them is a good place to start. Just a stroll through the garden every day is all it takes. If you're leaving for vacation, cover exposed soil with layers of newspaper or mulch. (The newspaper will eventually decompose.)

FEEDING

Continue to sidedress with a 10-10-10 fertilizer every 3 to 4 weeks.

WATERING

Now more than ever, plants and produce need their water. As fruits grow, a consistent watering schedule is very important.

MULCHING BEATS THE HEAT AND THE WEEDS

There aren't too many ways to escape the heat of the summer. Days can be hot and dry, two deadly ingredients for plants. Protecting your plants from both requires mulch. Mulch laid thickly enough helps retain moisture (which can be a life saver), cools the soil, and prevents weeds. And the greatest part about mulch—it's easy to find and in some cases costs next to nothing. Whatever mulch you select, the key is to be very generous. A 3 to 4 inch layer is necessary to do the trick.

There are many materials that make great mulch:

- *Bark chips: excellent because they don't break down quickly.*

- *Grass clippings: available weekly, break down quickly, and add nitrogen to the soil. Avoid thick layers, as they can smell as they break down.*

- *Shredded bark: personally my favorite; looks very natural and breaks down quickly. It will have to be replaced every year.*

- *Pine needles: great for acid-soil plants such as azaleas, rhododendrons, and blueberries.*

- *Leaves: widely available in the fall; work well, but break down quickly. Great for enriching the soil. To keep leaves from matting down, chop first with lawn mower.*

- *Compost: make your own, check your city or county compost pile, or purchase from garden centers.*

- *Rock: I see it all over the Midwest. I don't like it. It does nothing to enrich the soil and often is used with plastic underneath, which suffocates plants.*

- *Cocoa hulls: these look and smell beautiful and break down very quickly. But I find they get moldy and slimy with too much water.*

- *Nut hulls: most work well, just finding them is the trick.*

BEWILDERED BY BLIGHT

Tomatoes are one of the most popular vegetables grown in America. But they're not without their problems. I'm talking specifically about blight. If your tomato plants had blight last year, chances are good they're going to get it again this year. There are several tomato blights caused by several fungi. Each usually starts in the soil and then spreads quickly up the leaves. Spots appear on the leaves and eventually they shrivel up and fall off.

The best way to prevent blight is to plant your tomatoes in a different location every year. If that's not an option, concentrate on minimizing the spread of blight. Keep the garden clean. Be sure to remove all the plant material at the end of the year because it will contain the spores that cause blight and will infect your tomatoes all over again next year.

Give your plants room to grow. Space them generously, as they need good air circulation. Poor air circulation contributes to too much moisture or humidity, creating a breeding ground for blight. And finally, add a thick layer of mulch around the tomato plant. Mulch is an excellent barrier that prevents blight spores from splashing up from the soil onto the plant. And when you water, do it around the base; avoid overhead sprinklers. Water deeply but infrequently—mornings are best.

Flower

Follow-up

Usually by midsummer the garden is in full bloom. Hopefully you've had enough rain and sunshine to keep the garden looking great. But let's face it, summer's heat can be quite stressful to the garden, making it look tired and downright ragged. Here are some tips to help beat the heat in your flower beds.

WATERING

Most flower gardens need about an inch of water a week to keep them well hydrated. Rain gauges or recycled tuna cans can help you measure the amount of rain. If Mother Nature isn't providing enough, you'll have to add the difference.

Watering in the early morning hours is best. In the cool morning air, less water is lost to evaporation so more reaches your plants. If you can, water at the base of the plant. This will direct the water to the roots and will also reduce the humidity around the foliage. Wet foliage is a breeding ground for disease. Watering slowly and deeply is always best for your plants.

WEEDING

Weeds will take over and rob the water and nutrients from your flowers. Keep them out! After you've pulled them, keep them out with a thick layer of mulch. Three to four inches of mulch will keep the soil loose and help block the sun to keep weed seeds from sprouting. The mulch also keeps the soil cool and helps retain water. I always use a natural mulch that will break down and enrich the soil.

Thirty minutes a day will keep weeds away.

PRUNING

Your pruning shears are another tool you'll need during the dog days of summer to keep your garden clean. Cut all the spent blooms from your perennials. Some perennials can be cut to the ground after they bloom. They will come back with nice green foliage. Annuals like sweet alyssum, lobelia, and pansies (if you live in a cooler climate) can tolerate and appreciate a severe cut in early July. This encourages plants to come back invigorated with a new flush of blooms to take you into the fall season. The taller annuals like nicotiana, some petunias, marigolds, etc. need to be deadheaded to continue producing beautiful blooms. Otherwise the plant will set seeds and shut off its flower production. By deadheading, you force the plant to continue racing to set seeds. That means more flowers for you to enjoy!

Keep the bugs away with insecticidal soap. Spray the tops and bottoms of the leaves as needed. See page 10 for a homemade recipe.

White Powder on Flowers, Trees, or Shrubs?

If you notice a white, powdery coating on the leaves of any of your plants in the garden it's probably powdery mildew, a common fungus. It thrives when you have hot, humid days and cool nights. It looks bad but usually won't kill the plant. To keep it from spreading, spray the plant with this nontoxic concoction:

HOMEMADE FUNGICIDE

- *1 tablespoon baking soda*
- *2½ teaspoons horticultural oil (buy from garden center) or vegetable oil*
- *1 gallon water*

Mix together and pour into a pressurized sprayer or large spray bottle. Spray the entire plant and repeat spraying every fourteen days.

Next spring, start the treatment early in the season when plants leaf out. Continue every fourteen days to keep powdery mildew away.

FLOWER BOUQUETS AND CENTERPIECES

One thing I've learned through the show *Rebecca's Garden* is that there are many tricks of the trade that can really make a difference in and out of the garden. This is especially true when it comes to flower arranging. I'm no expert, but I'm learning.

Here are some tips:

Where will the flower piece go? This is very important when selecting flower heights.

Before heading out to your garden or the floral shop to purchase flowers, take a napkin that will be on your table or a pillow that decorates a room. This way you can choose flowers to match the theme of the room or table. The color of the flowers will depict a theme or feeling. Soft pastel colors give more of an English cottage feel. Very bold colors with brighter tones may give a more rustic feel.

The container is important, too. Ginger jars will create a wider spread of flowers, whereas a taller vase might work better on a buffet table by taking up less space. A rose bowl is beautiful for the center of the table. Flowers gracefully drape over its sides, and because it's shal-

low the flowers remain low so they won't block the face of the person sitting across from you. The only problem with the ginger jar is that if you simply place flowers and greens in it they flop over— it doesn't work. Which leads to one very simple but functional trick with transparent tape. Make an open grid with the tape over the top of the ginger jar. This will help to anchor and secure the stems of the flowers and greens.

To make a nice arrangement, start with the greenery. Place each piece around the container. Allow some to gently drape over the side and put some in the center. This sets the stage for the flowers. Starting with the tallest flowers, establish the height of the arrangement. Then add the rest of the flowers. Working with three colors will keep the arrangement from looking busy and messy. Also, always add a filler flower. These are light, airy, multi-branching flowers or greens such as baby's-breath or Queen-Anne's-lace. This helps to connect the whole arrangement.

If you want to make a bouquet without a vase, arrange the flowers on a flat surface rather than holding them in your hand. This way you'll have more control.

Start with the greens to establish the shape of the bouquet. Then start layering the flowers. Make sure they're different lengths. Every few layers add more of the greens. Use your more open flowers toward the bottom of the arrangement, near the bow. When you're finished, tie the arrangement together with a thick mass of raffia. And there you are—a beautiful bouquet that looks professionally done.

Size up your flowers. When arranging flowers in vases or containers, a good rule of thumb is that the flowers should be no more than two-thirds taller than the vase or container.

There's nothing like a vase of fresh flowers, but sometimes the pollen in the flowers can be a nuisance. Before placing the flowers on the table, clean the center of each flower with a pipe cleaner. One sweep around the pollen-coated anthers and the pollen will cling to the pipe cleaner instead of your linen tablecloth.

Nasturtiums are a spicy edible. Not only do they look good, they taste good too! The fiery flowers have a spicy flare that adds zing to soups, salads, and pastas. The young leaves are great eating when tossed into a salad. The seeds nasturtiums produce can be picked and pickled when green to use as a caper substitute.

SENSATIONAL SUNFLOWERS

These flowers are the smiling icons of the garden. Sunflowers have been around for years, and now more than ever, they are making a comeback. The sunflower is one of the many flowers native to North America and used completely by early North American Indians.

Planting

Sunflowers are planted from seeds directly into the garden once soil temperatures are close to 50°F. They prefer sunny locations and aren't picky about soil. Bury seeds about 1 to 2 inches deep and space about 12 inches apart (though I tend to cheat with spacing since my garden soil is very light and winds can be quite strong). Most seeds will germinate in about one to two weeks and take eighty to ninety days to reach maturity. If your garden suffers from cutworm attacks, be sure to surround the seedling with either coffee stir sticks, nails, collars from paper cups, or tuna cans with both ends removed. Sunflowers like plenty to drink as long as they don't sit in water. Watering is especially critical during the flowering stage. And fertilizer is a must, although be careful on the nitrogen—too much adds to the green growth but hinders flower development.

Harvesting

If you're growing sunflowers for cut flowers, harvest early in the morning. Choose flowers that have opened about one-third of the way. They will continue to open as they sit in a vase of water. If you're growing sunflowers for seeds, let the flowers continue. Eventually the heads will droop. When the back of the drooping seed head turns from green to yellow, then brown, you know it's time to harvest the head.

During this change, birds will flock to this flower feeder. If you want to keep them out, surround or cover the sunflower head with netting or cheesecloth. Personally, I enjoy watching the birds feast on the seeds and haven't really lost a lot of seeds. To harvest for drying, cut the stem 12 inches down from the head. Hang the head in a dry, airy location. When it is dry, you can extract the seed

by either gently rubbing the head with your hand or using a nice stiff wire brush. You'll get a lot of chaff so be prepared to winnow.

ROASTED SUNFLOWER SEEDS

- *unshelled sunflower seeds*
- *2 quarts water*
- *½ cup salt*
- *butter (optional)*
- *Worcestershire or teriyaki sauce (optional)*

Fill the bottom of a large saucepan with unshelled sunflower seeds. Add water and salt. Bring to a boil, reduce heat, and simmer for 2 hours. Drain seeds and spread out on a paper towel. Let them sit overnight.

To roast the seeds, spread them on a cookie sheet and bake at 325°F for about 25 to 40 minutes, until the seeds begin to slightly brown. The seeds are ready to eat. If you want a more fattening treat, toss the warm seeds in some butter. Other alternatives include flavoring the butter with a dash or two of either Worcestershire sauce or teriyaki sauce. In any case the seeds will be a delightful and nutrious snack.

Shrub and Lawn Follow-up

Summer heat can take its toll on lawns. You can help the lawn by keeping it well watered. During the summer, most lawns need about 1 to 2 inches of water a week. Watering in the morning is best. During the day, winds and the heat increase evaporation dramatically. Watering for longer periods of time will help water get to the root system. The soil becomes moist at deeper levels to encourage deep, drought-resistant roots. Infrequent, shallow watering will discourage the roots from growing deep into the soil, and roots will dry out much more quickly

Don't fertilize now. You don't want to encourage new growth when the grass is struggling with the heat.

Allow the grass to grow to 3 inches. The longer blades will shade the soil, keeping it cooler and helping it retain more moisture.

Overall, shrubs don't need a lot of attention. But during hot spells and when the shrub is blooming or producing fruit, you should water two to three times a week. Mulching around shrubs will help to retain more moisture. And during the spring and summer, you can fertilize shrubs once a month with a water soluble fertilizer.

MOW CIRCLES AROUND TREES

It's a pain to mow around trees. But it's more painful to the tree if the mower blade takes a chunk out of it. Just under the tree's bark is a cellular layer called the cambium. This is the tree's pipeline for water and nutrients. So don't cut into it. To prevent damage, remove the grass from around the trunk. Plant shade-tolerant flowers or add a thick layer of mulch. If you slip with the Weed-wacker, the flowers can be replaced—the tree can't.

Ornamental

Grasses

Although they've been around for centuries, ornamental grasses are finally gaining popularity across the country. They offer a display of color and texture year round. The season starts with slender spikes of green darting for the sky. By midsummer flowers unfold from the spikes. The flowers are like soft delicate feathers that gracefully sway and whistle in the wind. During fall, the foliage slowly fades from green to a light caramel. The flowers wither and fade, but hang tight to their stems. Not until they stand boldly above the snow covered landscape are the grasses really appreciated. This is just one reason to grow ornamental grasses. The other reasons include their diversity in color, texture, height, and form. And they're easy to grow and maintain.

PLANNING

Since most ornamental grasses are perennials, you must carefully consider the location where they will grow because you won't be moving them. Also you must consider your space allocation. There are two types of grasses. Those that spread in width as they grow are appropriately called "spreaders." And those that stay put and grow in clumps are sometimes referred to as "clumpers."

PLANTING

These plants love the sun but will tolerate some shade. The soil should be rich in organic matter. If yours isn't, amend the soil with compost, rotted manure, and peat moss. This is an important step since you won't be disturbing the soil once the grass is planted. Most grasses can be bought in containers. Place them in the soil as deep as they were in the container. Then water well. Like your lawn, ornamental grasses like to be fed with a fertilizer high in nitro-

Ten Easy Ornamental Grasses to Get You Started

These are all perennial within the listed zones; you can grow the tender types as annuals in colder zones.

TALL VARIETIES	ZONES	HEIGHT
Clump bamboo	4–9	8–10 ft.
Switch grass	5–10	3–8 ft.
Maiden grass	5–10	5–6 ft.
Northern sea oats	4–9	1–3 ft.
Fountain grass	5–9	2–4 ft.
Feather reed grass	5–10	3–5 ft.
Pampas grass	7–10	4–20 ft.
Purple moor grass	5–8	1^1/$_2$–2 ft.

SMALLER ORNAMENTAL GRASSES		
Blue fescue	4–10	6–12 in.
Japanese blood grass	5–10	10–18 in.

gen. Thereafter water as necessary, but remember these plants can go weeks without a watering. That's an important consideration for dry areas.

MAINTENANCE

There's not much these plants need: just water and fertilizer. In the late winter the grasses will need to be sheared down to make way for fresh spring growth. Tall grasses should be cut down, leaving 6 to 8 inches. Small grasses can be cut back to 1 to 2 inches. Save the trimmings and use as mulch or toss in the compost pile.

Water Gardens

If you've ever sat next to a babbling creek or a lapping lake, you already know the value of water in the landscape. Moving water puts us into a hypnotic state of relaxation. Not much else can be heard. For that reason, water gardens are becoming a valued addition to the landscape. People are also finding this a very low maintenance garden. It is versatile and can be placed just about anywhere. The size and shape is completely open to your creativity. And the plants that grow in water gardens are just fine without your fussing over them.

The tools and materials needed for a water garden are few:

- *a pool liner (either a hard plastic preformed liner or a flexible pond liner)*

- *a pump and tubing (if electronic pump, also need ground-fault interrupter outlet and long extension cord)*

- *water plants (oxygenators, deepwater plants, marginals, and surface floaters)*

- *shovel*

- *sand*

- *hose*

- *water*
- *flour and funnel (or hose)*

The look of a pond may seem hard to replicate, but you'd be surprised at just how easy it really is. Take it from me. I've built a simple one and continue to upgrade it every year. Now I'm in the process of building a two-tiered water garden, waterfall included. If I can do it, so can you.

DESIGNING

First pick a location. Easy enough. Any considerations? Yes! Before digging in, check with the utility companies to find all underground wires. Obviously, keep the pond away from these. The type of plants you put in the garden will determine how much sun the pond will get. Keep in mind that partial sun is fine for most water plants.

Second, outline the pool. If you're using a hard, preformed pool, turn it upside down and trace its shape using flour sprinkled through a funnel. Or a rope works just as well. A flexible pond liner gives you the green light to be creative. Once you've completed the outline, stand back, walk around the yard, and look out the windows of your house to make sure it's exactly what you want. I even recommend taking a day or two before you dig to make sure the pond will be where you want it.

BUILDING

Get digging, using the flour or rope as your guide. Ponds can vary in depth; it all depends on what your expectations are and if you have children. Two feet deep is perfectly adequate. Around the edge of the outline dig down about 6 inches. Then make a ledge about 8 to 10 inches wide for water plants. The ledge can surround the whole pond or you can have it vary in location. If you don't make a ledge, you'll have to come up with a creative way of raising your plants under water (stacking bricks, etc.). The ledge is much better.

From the ledge continue digging down to a depth of at least 18 inches. Get rid of all the soil, any sharp rocks, and any other surprises left behind from nature or a builder. The goal is to have a completely smooth hole. To ensure smoothness, add sand thick enough to cushion any rough edges. If you have a preformed pool, you can now drop it in and fill in around the edges. The liner is a little more tricky. Think of this as lining a pie tin with pie crust. Start with the center and bottom of the pond. Pull and tuck the liner to fit smoothly and securely, filling all crevices. You want all the edges smooth. If you've designed a creative shape, you'll have to gather the liner, making folds to allow it to fit well. Just make sure you make the folds as precisely as possible, since excess gathering

or buckling will destroy the natural look of the pond. The liner should overlap the top edge of the pond by at least 8 inches. This will give you room for changes.

At this point, I like to fill the garden with water. The weight of the water will pull down the excess liner to help fill in small crevices. Let the water sit overnight—go in and relax, it's been a hard day. The next day you can then safely cut away the excess liner over the rim of the water garden. But leave about a 6-inch overlap. Hide the liner overlap with rocks, stones, and plants.

To add the sound of running water you'll need a pump. Garden centers sell them; choose pumps by how much water you want to move in one hour. The cheapest pumps are good for circulating the water, and with some tubing you can create a stream of water to cascade over the stones and into the water. The larger, more expensive pumps are for ponds that need some muscle to carry the water up to a waterfall or for a dramatic spray or fountain. What you choose is up to you; the placement is all the same. The pump needs to be submerged and placed either on the bottom of the pond or on top of blocks. (The pump must be covered with water at all times.) On the side of the pump will be a spigot to which flexible plastic tubing can be attached. Attach a tube and run it along the bottom of the pond and up the sides. You'll need some lightweight stones to anchor the tubing in place without constricting the flow of water. Allow enough tubing to carry the water up the sides of the pond to the highest point. Again, anchor and hide the tubing in the process. The electrical cord on the pump will need hiding too. Tuck it against the pool wall, using rock to hold it in place. Then run the cord

Summer

along the side of the pool to the outlet. I hide my cord with a thick layer of mulch.

ADDING PLANTS

The next step is to add plants. This will give the pond the final feature that makes it the focal point in any garden. Plants not only look good but are necessary to keep the pond water in balance. There are many to choose from. Most are hardy or tropical and are grouped according to their characteristics.

Oxygenators are a must for any pond. They grow underwater, working hard to keep the water clean. They control algae and give off oxygen for the fish. You'll need one bunch of oxygenators for every 1 to 2 square feet. Eel grass is a good oxygenator to try.

Bog plants love wet feet. These plants will do well around the pool as long as the soil doesn't dry out. If you want them in the pool, they must be left in the container with a layer of gravel over the soil's surface to keep the soil from washing into the pool. These plants should be submerged no deeper than six inches.

Marginal plants are like bog plants; they love water. But these plants grow in the water around the edge of the pond. This is the purpose of the ledges. Marginal plants, such as the water iris, are excellent for adding height and texture to the garden.

Aquatics are the floating plants. Their foliage floats on the water's surface while the roots dangle below. Some are free floating, while others, like lilies, are anchored in a container. They can help reduce algae. Don't cover the entire water surface with floaters or oxygenators or aquatic animals will suffer.

To keep your water garden looking great, prune dead leaves and blooms from your water plants regularly. Remove any stringy algae. Thin out or divide overgrown plants in late spring or early fall.

> *It is important to wait up to two days before adding plants or fish. Your goal should be to cover up to 60 percent of the water surface with plants.*

ADDING WILDLIFE

Water snails are a great way to keep algae under control and keep your pond water well balanced. And here's another good one: foraging fish control pests. They eat aphids, flies, and mosquito larvae, as well as algae. Fish are a great source of carbon dioxide and nitrogen. Goldfish are as good because they add color. For every 9 square feet of surface area, add about twelve water snails and two 3 to 5 inch goldfish.

WHISKEY BARREL WATER GARDENS

You don't need to have a lot of space to have a water garden. Even those with the tightest living quarters can enjoy the sound of running water. Make your garden in a whiskey barrel, or a plastic half-barrel. Whiskey barrels can be purchased from the garden center. Just make sure it's a real half-barrel whiskey barrel. Many places will sell what looks like a whiskey barrel, but really isn't. When wet, the real whiskey barrels are tightly sealed, and no water leaks out. Fake ones are made of cheaper wood and don't work.

Start by filling the barrel up with water. Let it sit for two days at least. This will allow the wood to absorb water and expand, filling any slight crack or crevice and making it watertight. If you're concerned about a release of any toxins from the alcohol, line the barrel with plastic pool liner. You won't need many plants to make this garden look nice. Just a few will do.

For the plants in containers like the water lilies and iris, you'll need to add a brick to the bottom of the barrel. This will place the plants near the surface and keep them from drowning. Continue adding plants until you get your desired look. And for an extra bonus, add a water pump. But don't pay the big-ticket price on the ones made for ponds. For these small container water gardens an aquarium pump will do the trick. It won't pull as much water, but for this small arrangement it will work just fine.

If you want a year-round garden, put your half-barrel on a plant caddy. When the temperatures get near the freezing point, roll the barrel indoors.

Summer
Projects

DRYING FLOWERS

After enjoying the flowers in your garden all spring and summer, you may want to stretch that beauty into fall. It's done by preserving the flowers or drying them. The results are fabulous, and the process is simple.

The first step is to pick the flowers at the right time—just before the flowers reach full bloom. If you wait too long, the flowers will not dry well. It's best to pick the flowers in the morning after the dew has dried. This is when the flowers are full of water and most plump.

Remove the leaves from the bottom of the stems. Gather together a small bunch and wrap the stems together with a rubber band. Hang upside down in a dark, dry location. After a week or so, the flowers should be dry.

WINDOW BOXES

Adding a window box to your home is like adding the perfect floral arrangement to a room. Not only does it accent the outside of the house, but also it's a warm invitation for all your visitors.

If you're going to add a box to your

window, it's important to make sure it fits. If the box is much longer than the window, it will look like a mustache. Too small, it will look like an eyebrow. Measure the width of the frame of the window and add a couple of inches on each side. You'll have a box that balances and frames the window nicely. If you don't build one yourself, you can purchase a variety of boxes. I prefer those made from cedar. They look natural, weather well, and can last a long time. Plastic is good as long as it's very strong and thick. Unfortunately, many of the plastic boxes I've seen tend to start sagging from the soil and water and can warp from the heat. Rod iron hay racks are very nice

and very sturdy. They need a natural fiber liner to hold the soil and plants in place. Whatever you choose, you must remember that for a window box to continue looking nice a bit of attention is required, sometimes on a daily basis. Here are some helpful hints:

I prefer using soil-less mixtures in my window boxes. These contain lots of peat moss, which is excellent for retaining water. If the box will be in a hard-to-reach location, mix slow-release fertilizer into the soil-less mixture before planting flowers. Otherwise I prefer to fertilize regularly with a water-soluble fertilizer. Then plant the flowers and greenery. And don't be shy, pack them in. You can

Summer

always remove some if quarters get too tight. When you pack them in, the flowers are forced to cascade over the sides of the box for a dramatic, eye-catching display of color. The plant selection is certainly up to you; just be sure to choose those whose sun requirements match your location. Also make sure the plants share the same water requirements. Mix in vining plants to cascade over the edges of your box.

THE PERFECT PICNIC

There's nothing quite like a perfect picnic to get you in a good mood. But before you pack your basket, cruise through your garden. You'd be surprised at the great things that are growing that can add a special touch to your open-air affair.

Don't leave without a handful of mint. Not only will it help keep bees away, but also a sprig or two in the lemonade will add a refreshing flavor. If you have potted herbs, they make a nice edible centerpiece. Everyone can snip off fresh herbs to add to his or her custom-toss salad. Dishes and bowls can be a drag to worry about. Make your own from the garden! A head of a cabbage hollowed out makes a delicious bowl for spinach dip or a fresh salad. And if your picnic takes you into the evening hours, don't forget citronella candles. Not only do they add romance and ambience, but they also help keep the mosquitoes away.

Summer Garden
Checklist

- *Don't mow short; taller grass keeps the lawn from drying out.*
- *Don't fertilize lawns now; wait until fall.*
- *Wait until the cooler temperatures of early fall to plant trees and shrubs.*
- *Move houseplants outside. Keep them in shade and gradually move to sun or the plant will get scorched.*
- *Stay ahead of the weeds—the number one pest in the garden.*
- *Remove spent blooms from annual flowers for continuous blooms.*
- *As temperature warms, mulch garden and flower beds.*
- *Pick flowers early in the morning for the best display.*
- *Pick beans daily for continuous harvest.*
- *Fertilize containers and window boxes every one to two weeks with diluted or half-strength fertilizer.*
- *Keep annuals deadheaded for continuous blooms.*

▲ It's payback time
Photo by Michelle Laurita, courtesy of Rebecca's Garden Magazine

▲ Dirt-y duty
Photo by Doug Beasley, courtesy of Rebecca's Garden Magazine

▲ A garden in "action"

▲ Lights, camera . . . and gardening

▲ Enjoying the late summer blooms
Photo by Doug Beasley, courtesy of Rebecca's Garden Magazine

Fall

. . . the harvest season

There's a nip in the air, signs of changing weather, a changing landscape, and a changing attitude, I'm sure. Just don't think that this is the time to sit back and relax—it's not. It's time to put some muscle into the garden. A lot of chores must be completed before the landscape changes its face. The vegetable garden is full of goodies to be picked, eaten, and preserved. As spring bulbs go in, summer bulbs come out. The gardens need cleaning, the soil needs amending—again. Trees and shrubs need protection from the wicked winds of the North and the lawns need fertilizing, mowing, and clearing (picking up dead leaves, rotten fruit, or blown-in debris). Whew, all this talk and I'm exhausted already! But trust me, the effort is worth it—you just have to wait until next spring to see the results. As my mother-in-law would say, "Definitely a character builder."

The biggest advantage of working in the fall garden is the explosion of vivid warm colors that wrap around you, as well as the nice weather—when it obliges! The potpourri of color woven into the landscape makes working outside irresistible.

Fall

Vegetable Care

Continue harvesting and enjoying the produce. Vegetables you can't eat right away can be frozen, dried, or canned. As the plants lose steam and start dying back, give them a new home in the compost pile as long as they are disease free.

As you pull stems and vines from the garden, be sure to mix in autumn leaves, compost, manure, etc., to enrich the soil. Make a list of where vegetables were growing so that next year you can rotate the crops and plant them in different locations.

TRICKS WITH TOMATOES

As the season winds down, you may need to jump-start the ripening process of your green tomatoes. You just have to get to the root of the matter. The tomato root, that is. Here's what to do:

Drive a garden fork into the soil 12 inches away from the stem of the tomato plant. Move the fork back and forth to loosen the soil as if you were in the process of digging up the tomato plant. This stresses the roots, which then sends a distress signal through the plant. The plant quits growing. The tomatoes quit growing. Instead, the plant will focus all its energy on ripening. In no time, the fruits will blush with color—but they won't get any bigger. Do this three to four weeks before the first anticipated frost to guarantee red tomatoes.

Ripen Tomatoes Without a Vine

If the forecast is flirting with frost, you'd better harvest your tomatoes. It takes only one cold night to bring down the entire crop. While picking, don't just reach for the red tomatoes, pick the yellow and green ones, too. With a little storage savvy you can save these and preserve the fresh taste of summer throughout most of fall. Here's how:

Eat the red tomatoes right away. The yellow ones can be left on the counter to ripen slowly. The green ones are for long-term storage. Pick through the bunch and remove any with blemishes. Although these tomatoes are hard, don't manhandle them. Any bruise will turn into rot in storage. Carefully place them in a shallow box or container that has been lined with newspaper. Don't let the tomatoes touch each other. Put the box of green tomatoes in a cool, dark location (the cooler the better, as long as temperatures remain above 38°F). Once a week check the tomatoes. If any start to rot, remove them and change the paper. As they start turning yellow, bring them up to the kitchen. Or when you're in the mood for fresh tomato slices, move some up to your kitchen counter and give them a week or more. They'll slowly ripen and will taste as if they were just picked from the garden!

Too many tomatoes? Clean and quarter them. Arrange on a cookie sheet, sprinkle with a bit of salt, and bake at 225°F. The tomatoes are done when they are shriveled and leathery without being dry. Generally they'll need to bake about 8 to 12 hours. Store in the freezer or airtight containers. Use them as a snack or in recipes that call for tomatoes. The concentrated flavor of dried tomatoes can't be beat!

FRIED GREEN TOMATOES

Don't knock them until you've tried them! These slices of green are really quite a treat. Here's what I do:

- *green tomatoes sliced about ⅓ inch thick*
- *seasoned croutons*
- *flour*
- *olive oil*
- *salt*
- *pepper*

Place a handful of croutons and about ⅓ cup of flour into a plastic zipper bag. Squeeze out the air and seal shut. Roll over the bag with a rolling pin to crush the croutons. Add three to four tomato slices and shake, coating both sides of each slice with breading. Pan fry in hot olive oil, just long enough to slightly brown the tomatoes. Remove to a platter, add salt and fresh-ground pepper. Enjoy!

HARVESTING CHIVES EVEN IN THE CHILLIEST WEATHER

One sure sign of spring comes from the tiny blades of chives as they start pushing through the soil. You know a fresh green salad can't be far behind. The mild onion flavor of chives adds spice to any soup, salad, or dish. And with this nifty technique you won't have to wait until spring to enjoy them. Here's how:

During the fall season as temperatures cool down, dig up a clump of chives and transplant into a container large enough to fit the root ball, adding soil if you have to. Since clay pots will crack in freezing temperatures, plant the chives in a plastic pot. That's it for now. Leave the potted chives outside to endure the elements. The tops will freeze and wither away, and eventually the roots will do the same. This sends the plant into the dormancy period it needs.

After about two to three months, bring the pot indoors and place it by a sunny window. As the plant thaws, water when necessary. In no time at all needles of green will start shooting out of the soil. Very soon you'll be harvesting the chives even if the calendar says you're not supposed to! Once they're about 6 inches tall, you can start snipping. Chives are best eaten fresh, but you can also enjoy their taste when they're frozen or dried.

GREENS

One thing I love about fall is the selection of cool-season vegetables available. Beets, radishes, and gourmet greens are the fixings that make a killer salad, the kind you find in gourmet restaurants for a hefty price. By using your pennies wisely you can grow your own gourmet greens for a fraction of the cost all season long. Here's how:

Purchase seeds. There are mesclun mixes that produce the kind of greens used in restaurants. The seeds are tiny so don't bury them any deeper than ¼ inch. I simply press them into the soil.

Watering can be tricky: too much, and you wash the seeds away; too little and they dry out. A gentle spray will keep the seeds in place until they germinate. Keep the water coming and in three weeks you'll be ready to start harvesting.

The trick to gourmet greens is a timely harvest. Cut the lettuce when it's about 3 inches high. This way the leaves are bite sized, ready to be eaten, and there's no need to tear or cut the leaves. Overgrown leaves taste bitter. Harvesting in the morning is best. Cut the greens about ½ inch above the soil, leaving some stem. This way the lettuce will continue growing. To get two or three more harvests, feed with diluted liquid fertilizer, such as fish emulsion, after you cut the plant. Wash the leaves under cold water and dry them with a paper towel. Store in the refrigerator.

For a variety of baby greens or mesclun, try growing the following:

- *arugula*
- *red mustard*
- *cress*
- *mizuna*
- *any leaf lettuces*
- *mustard*

GREEN MANURE

It's not what you think! Green manure is a fun garden term for plants that are grown to enrich the soil. It's a great method for amending the soil after crops deplete it of nutrients. Green manures, sometimes called cover crops, are used by many farmers and gardeners across the country. This manure is nothing more than grains like buckwheat, annual rye, or clover that are grown to be purposely turned under before they mature. Besides adding nutrients, green manures prevent soil erosion and act as a living mulch.

You can get seeds for green manures at some garden centers. Otherwise check the mail-order catalogues of local stores.

Sow the grains directly into the soil in the fall after the harvest. When planting, clear the area of all garden debris. Mix in peat, compost, and manure for added benefit. Plant the seeds as you would lawn seeds, water, and wait. The green manure should not be allowed to mature; turn it under before seeds form. In warmer climates the green manure will grow into the winter season and can then be tilled under. In colder areas the plants will die back and can be tilled under in the spring.

PRIME TIME FOR PUMPKINS

Knowing what to look for is critical when picking your perfect pumpkin. If you didn't grow your own, don't worry. Pumpkin growing is big business. You're bound to find a farm where you can pick your own. The obvious tip is to look for an orange pumpkin. If there's a tinge of green it's not a big deal; the pumpkin will continue to ripen after you've brought it home. Look for the size and shape you want—these two qualities will not change. The skin of the shimmering orange globe should be smooth without deep scars.

If you're picking from the vine, be very careful to keep 3 to 4 inches of stem intact. Otherwise the pumpkin will be more susceptible to rot.

Once you get the pumpkin home what do you do with it? Keep it warm! It will stay fresh longer when the temperature is warm. It's Jack Frost nipping at its nose that doesn't sit well with a pumpkin. Either cover the pumpkin or bring it indoors on frosty nights.

If you plan to carve the pumpkin, save the seeds. Toasted they make a great treat. Wash and spread them on a cookie sheet. You may sprinkle with salt. Bake at 350°F until they turn golden brown, usually 10 to 15 minutes.

> *To keep your newly carved pumpkin from shriveling, coat the cut edges with petroleum jelly. This will help seal in the moisture.*

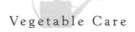

Fall

Flower Care

PERENNIALS

At the end of the season remove any foliage or stems that are infested with insects or disease. Trim the plants down as they die back. As nighttime temperatures drop below freezing and the ground begins to freeze as well, cover plants with a thick layer of mulch. You can use wood chips, straw, evergreen boughs, or chopped leaves. Otherwise, the freezing and thawing soil will kill the plant. If perennial beds are located under the eaves of your home, make sure the gutters are kept clear to keep over-flowing water from drowning your plants.

ANNUALS

As they die back, pull them out and throw them in the compost pile. You can enrich soil in annual beds over winter with an inch of compost or other soft mulch, or with a cold-loving green manure (oats, winter rye, hairy vetch).

Overwintering Geraniums

One of the most popular flowers grown in the United States is the geranium.

Most of us grow them as annuals even though in warmer climates they can be grown year-round. In areas where the temperatures dip below freezing, you can overwinter the plants to use season after season.

Before the first frost dig up the entire geranium plant. Put it in a bushel basket or large container. Let the plant dry out, roots and all. When the soil is completely dry, shake the plant or gently knock off all the soil. If the leaves have dried, remove them (or just leave them, they'll eventually die and fall off). Place the plant in a large paper bag, and then tie it up with string or a rubber band. Store in a cool, dark, and dry room. Every couple of weeks take a peek. If you see a bit of mold growing on the plant's stems, it's too wet. Open up the sack and let the plant dry out. If the stem is shriveled, it's too dry. With a spray bottle lightly mist the plant. Recheck it in another week. Continue peeking at the plant throughout the winter.

In late winter pot the geranium in good potting soil. Cut the main stem back to a couple of inches, water well, and set the plant in a sunny location. Eventually the plant will start growing. When there is no more threat of frost, move the geranium outdoors.

For fantastic fall color, plant ornamental kale or flowering cabbage. As the temperature gets colder, the color gets bolder. And the leaves can be used as a garnish for hors d'oeuvres or salads. Both the kale and cabbage can be eaten steamed.

Flowers of Frost

Don't let the cooler temperatures rob your garden of color. There are many flowers that actually rise to the occasion when there's a nip in the air.

Aster	*Sedum 'Autumn Joy'*
Chrysanthemum	*Ornamental kale or flowering cabbage*
Scabiosa	*Sunflower*
Japanese anemone	*Pansy*

So plant some of these flowers in the summer and enjoy their beauty late in the fall.

Bulbs for All Seasons

SPRING BULBS

One of the most encouraging spring sights is brilliant purple crocus poking their heads out from under the snow-covered landscape. Not long after the crocus come daffodils, tulips, and hyacinths. If you want spring bulb bouquets, now's the time to get them planted.

Preparing Soil

Since the bulbs will be undisturbed for years, it's important to enrich the soil prior to planting. Bulbs prefer well-drained soil. Mix in compost, rotted manure, peat moss, or leaf mold to improve soil drainage. Let the area sit and settle while you go shopping for bulbs.

Bulbs emerge at differing times of the spring. With a little preplanning you can orchestrate a symphony of color that will take you right through spring.

Selecting

Don't be cheap. Buy good quality. In the bulb department, you really get what you pay for. Stay away from bulbs with deep scars, bruises, soft spots, or mold. If the bulb is shriveled, it's not good. It should be solid and firm and feel heavy for its size. Don't worry about the condition of the onion-like skin; some bulbs will have intact skins, but other skins may be loose or even missing.

Once you've purchased the bulbs, it's best to plant them right away. If that's impossible, they must be stored in a cool, dry location like a refrigerator. Just make sure you store them in either a paper bag or plastic bags with holes, as airtight bags encourage rotting and mold.

Planting

The size of the bulb and the soil type determine how deep each bulb must be planted. A good rule of thumb is to dig the hole three times deeper than the diameter of the bulb; the bigger the bulb, the deeper it should be planted.

Adjust recommended planting depths to match your soil type. Sandy soil: the hole should be 1 to 2 inches deeper. Clay soils: reduce the depth by an inch or two.

Bulbs can be planted separately or in clusters. At the base of each hole, mix in a handful of bulb foods or a timed-release fertilizer high in potassium. Place the bulbs in the hole with their points up. Cover with soil and soak the area with water. Once the weather stays cold add an insulating layer of mulch to prevent abrupt changes in soil temperature during the late fall and early spring.

and match a variety of bulbs for the most spectacular bouquets. If only we could get that same prearranged look in our garden. Well you can! The trick is to layer your bulbs when you plant them. By layering you can create an arrangement of flowers that's sure to get the neighbors talking! Here's how:

SHOPPING LIST

- variety of bulbs—big and small with differing blooming times. (I use daffodils, a variety of tulips, grape hyacinths, scillas, snowdrops, and crocuses.)
- bulb food

STEP-BY-STEP: LAYERING

- *Divide the bulbs according to size.*
- *Dig a hole deep enough to accommodate the largest bulbs. Remember, hole depth should be three to four times the diameter of the bulb.*
- *Scratch bulb food into the bottom of the hole.*
- *Place the largest bulbs into the hole, roots down, points up.*
- *Cover the first layer of bulbs, leaving the very tips of the bulbs exposed.*
- *Repeat the process using the next larger size of bulbs: scratch in fertilizer, place bulbs, and cover with soil.*
- *Continue until you have a layer cake*

Planting Depths for Bulbs

BULBS	PLANTING DEPTH (INCHES)
Daffodils	8–10
Tulips	4–10
Hyacinths	6–8
Crocuses	1–2

Layering Spring Bulbs

Blooming spring bulbs herald the beginning of warmth. They look beautiful in the yard, but not as beautiful as what a florist can do in a vase. Florists can mix

of bulbs with the smallest ones on top.

- *When the ground freezes cover the surface with 3 to 5 inches of mulch.*
- *Your job is done. Next spring the bulbs will treat you to a dramatic huge vase of flowers.*

SUMMER BULBS

If you planted corms, rhizomes, or tubers late last spring you planted summer bulbs, even though these are not "true" bulbs. Here's the difference:

Bulbs: Round or oval-shaped encased flower buds. They are made up of fleshy layers, like an onion, with roots on the bottom.

Corms: Harder than bulbs and don't have layers or scales like a true bulb. Unlike the bulb, which may live indefinitely by splitting up, the corm withers and dies after a year of growth but is replaced by new corms that usually grow on top of the existing corm.

Tubers: Look like swollen stems or roots. They have leaf buds or "eyes" over their surface. The tuber stores plant food to support new shoots.

Rhizomes: Thick fleshy roots that grow horizontally near the soil surface.

Most summer bulbs are wimps when it comes to cold weather and will die if left in the ground. So if you live where temperatures drop below 32°F, you'll have to dig up the summer bulbs and store them indoors until next spring. But timing is everything. Don't get too hasty. If the foliage is still green, the bulbs are continuing to store food for next year's bloom. Once they turn yellow it's time. Carefully dig up the plants and remove the soil. Cut any foliage still clinging to the bulbs. Allow them to dry in a cool location for twenty-four hours. Gladiolus need to dry for three weeks.

After digging up dahlias, cannas, callas, or caladiums, place the bulbs with their foliages in a well-ventilated area that's about 60° to 70°F. Let them dry for one to three days.

Storing

Bury the bulb in a box of peat moss, vermiculite, or sand. Spread the bulbs apart and cover. (Make sure you include a label so you'll remember what you've stored.) Store in a cool, dry location. Every couple of weeks take a peek. If the bulbs are shriveled, it's too dry. Mist them with water. If you see or smell mold, it's too wet. Open the box and let them dry in the dark. If the basement is damp, move them to a drier location. If they start sprouting, too much light is getting in.

FORCING BULBS IN WINTER

Those of you who just can't wait for spring blooms can trick the bulbs. With a little timing savvy, you can enjoy spring bouquets for any upcoming winter event. Technically, it's called forcing. The tricky part comes in the timing. Bulbs need cold storage to bloom. Tulips need about fourteen to twenty weeks, daffodils need sixteen to twenty-two weeks, hyacinths ten to fourteen weeks, and crocuses, snowdrops, and smaller bulbs need twelve weeks of cold storage.

The first step is planting. Place small bulbs close together in a 6-inch pot. Then cover with potting soils, leaving the noses, or points, just barely exposed. Water immediately after planting and keep the soil moist. The entire pot should then be placed in a cool dark environment where temperatures are at least 35° to 40°F, no colder! Then sit back and mark your calendar. Before you know it, the stems will emerge almost on cue. When they're about an inch tall, bring them up to a brightly lit, cool room. (Temperatures above 50°F cause the flowers to grow quickly and become spindly.)

Quick-Blooming Bulbs

Amaryllis and paperwhite narcissus sport blooms in just four to six weeks and don't need the cold storage that other bulbs require.

Paperwhite narcissus bulbs produce petite white flowers that sit on top of tall, slender stalks. The flowers have a strong fragrance that will fill a room. It takes six weeks from planting to blooming.

To plant, put a layer of gravel in the bottom of a shallow pot. Pack the bulbs tightly into the pot and cover with more gravel. Add water until it just touches the bases of the bulbs (deeper water can encourage rotting). Water regularly and don't let bulbs dry out. Keep blooming plants away from direct sunlight. Temperatures between 60° and 65°F are ideal for paperwhites. Cool climates encourage stronger growth and longer-lasting blooms. (After bloom, discard bulbs, as they won't bloom successfully the next year.)

If you want continuous flowers, plant a pot of bulbs every week.

Amaryllis is another quick bloomer. This bulb produces up to four large, dramatic flowers on a single tall stem. When you're shopping, remember that the bigger the bulb, the more flowers it will produce.

Place the bulb into a pot partly filled with potting soil. Spread the roots and bury, leaving the upper one-third of the bulb exposed. Water after planting, but don't soak, then hold off on the water for two weeks. After that water sparingly. Place the container in a shaded, warm place (70° to 75°F). When the flower stalk stands 6 to 8 inches tall, move the plant to a brighter location. Now, just sit back and get ready for an exquisite display. After the bloom, don't throw the amaryllis out. Treat as a houseplant and then move the plant outdoors in the summer. By Labor Day, dig up the bulb and store in a cool, dark basement. Do not water for two months. Cut the dead foliage, replant, and start the process all over again!

Bringing Houseplants Indoors

If you treated your houseplants to a backyard summer vacation, now it's time to bring them back indoors. It takes only one chilly night to ruin a houseplant. But there are some precautions you should take when bringing the plants back indoors. There's always a chance that tiny insects like mites or aphids may have taken up residence on the plant. Inside the house, these insects will multiply and move on to other plants.

Here's what you need to do: Examine the plant carefully, paying close attention to the undersides of the leaves. If you see any pests, remove them. But just to be safe, spray the entire plant with insecticidal soap. Then bring the plant indoors and isolate it from any other houseplants for two weeks. This way if there's a problem you can take care of it before it spreads.

Fall

Fall Tree and Shrub Care

Fall is tree and shrub time. As flowers fade, trees and shrubs with colorful leaves take center stage in the theater of seasons. Their vivid tapestry warms our spirits and often makes us think of favorite pastimes—high school football games, camping, and just being outside enjoying fall colors with family. So spread the spirit, plant a tree!

Fall is an excellent time to plant trees and shrubs as long as you do it early. The plants need to establish some roots before the soil freezes. Try to get shrubs and trees in at least six weeks before the first frost. Watch the garden centers for great markdown prices. The rules are the same when planting trees and shrubs in the fall as during the spring. Making the right choices can bring a riot of color into your garden as the seasons change.

The following plants will start the fall garden on fire:

Trees: Red maple, quaking aspen (for colder climates), ginkgo, and sweet gum (for warmer climates)

Shrubs: Witchhazel, burning bush, and blueberries

WINTER PREPARATION

Winter weather can take a harsh toll on the plants in your landscape. With some advanced preparation you can boost the plant's likelihood of surviving even the most severe conditions.

Protecting Shrubs

Any tree or shrub that maintains its leaves during the winter is an evergreen. It's very important to make sure they're pumped up with water before winter sets in. During the fall season water all your evergreens thoroughly and deeply until you have a hard freeze. The best way is to lay a hose with a slow stream of water at the base of the plant. Allow the hose to run for about thirty minutes a day for shrubs and one to two hours for trees.

Nothing can bring down a branch from a shrub faster than a heavy load of ice or snow. To protect upright shrubs like arborvitae, wrap them with strips of burlap starting from the bottom up. The wrapping helps to keep the branches from bending and breaking from the weight of heavy snow or ice.

For more sensitive evergreen shrubs (dwarf Alberta spruce, rhododendron, and azalea), the goal is to protect the plant from wind and provide shade from the winter sun. You can do this effectively by caging the plant with burlap. Place stakes all around and about 12 inches from the plant. Cut burlap to match the height of the plant and wrap it around the stakes, leaving a 6-inch gap from the ground to aid in air circulation. Secure the burlap. (The top will be left open.) Then fill the inside with leaves for added insulation.

No flowers on your shrubs? You probably cut off their heads! Shrubs that flower early in the spring form their buds from midsummer through fall. Don't prune them in fall or you'll lose your flowers.

Winterizing Trees

Trees are pretty hardy, even in the worst winter conditions. But for new trees wind can bring death in a snap. If your tree is in a windy area, stake it for its first year. If you keep mulch around the tree, pull the mulch at least 12 inches away from the trunk to discourage rodent damage. If rabbits and deer present a problem, wrap loose cages of chicken wire around and 12 inches from trunks.

All new trees that have trunks less than 6 to 8 inches in diameter need to be wrapped. Their thin skin is especially sensitive to the sun. The sun warms and thaws the trunk during the day, but at night it freezes, causing the trunk to split or crack. This is called sunscald. The crack could expose the tree to all kinds of diseases and insects and can stunt its growth. You can prevent sunscald by wrapping the trunk with strips of burlap or commercial tree wrap, hardware cloth, or plastic trunk protector, which often comes with new trees or can be purchased. Starting 1 inch below the ground, wrap 18 inches of the trunk. The wrap should be removed in the spring once temperatures begin to warm steadily.

As far as pruning goes, don't do anything except remove dead branches until the tree is completely dormant. Or wait until early spring.

Fall

Lawn Care

Early fall is an excellent time to start or repair a lawn. The same rules apply as if you were doing it in the spring. But it's important to get the job done early. The new turf needs time to establish roots before the ground freezes.

AERATING

Think of aerating your lawn as "unplugging" your soil. It's the "Roto-Rooter" of yard work, and I think it's one of the best things you can do for your lawn. You'll need a lawn aerator to get the job done. Most rental agencies have them, or check a local hardware store. The machine is big and quite heavy so call a few friends over to help.

An aerator has a large drum covered with hollow spikes. As you push the machine across the lawn, the spikes are driven into the soil. It then spits back out 6-inch cores of soil across the lawn. It's not a pretty sight, but your lawn will love it. Aeration helps open up the lawn, allowing oxygen and water to get to the root zone. It works especially well on lawns with clay, compacted soils, and those with thatch buildup.

To do a thorough job of aerating,

make several passes with the core-munching machine. Go back and forth and then crosswise over the lawn. When your neighbor comes running out of his house with his mouth wide open screaming, "What have you done to your grass?" you'll know your job is complete.

The soil cores look messy, but leave them on the grass. Eventually they'll break down, if the lawn mower doesn't chew them up first. Aeration should be done at least once a year if not twice. It's best to do it in fall and then again in the spring.

FALL FEEDING

The very best time to fertilize is in the fall. Even if you don't fertilize your grass throughout the year, do it in the fall. Many companies offer "winterizing" lawn food, which is good. You don't really want a fertilizer that promotes a lot of top growth. Instead you want one that will nourish and strengthen the roots for winter. By fertilizing in the fall, your lawn will be the first to green up in the spring.

MAINTAINING LAWN MOWERS

As the growing season comes to an end, we're so busy putting our lawns and gardens to bed that we forget about the tools we've used all season, like the lawn mower. By taking some easy maintenance steps now you can assure everything is in tip-top shape for next spring. A little proactive winterizing maintenance will save yourself a lot of reactive repair later.

- *With the engine off, remove the wire from the spark plug. Drain the gasoline according to instructions in the manual (fuel left over the winter becomes gummy).*

- *Reconnect the spark plug wire and start the engine, using the small amount of gasoline left in the carburetor. Allow the machine to idle until it stops. Let the engine cool and disconnect the spark plug wire again. Drain the crankcase, making sure to reseal it so dirt can't enter the engine.*

- *With the spark plug still disconnected, tip the mower on its side and remove dirt or grass clippings by spraying with a garden hose. Scrape out any remaining grass residue with a brush or paint scraper. The underside of the steel deck may need a new paint job to prevent rusting.*

- *Check the blade for condition and sharpness. If the blade requires sharpening, follow the blade maintenance procedure in the operator's manual. Make sure the blade is balanced before you reinstall and tighten it. A simple way to balance a blade is to put a round-shank screwdriver through the center hole and hold the blade upright. If the blade tips, grind off a little metal from the "low" side. Rotary lawn mower blades should be sharpened on the upper surface only.*

- *With the mower right side up, clean off all the dirt, grime, and grass clippings from the external parts of the engine and top of the mower. Give special attention to the cylinder head fins and blower housing, which must be completely clean for proper air cooling.*

- *Now service the spark plug. If needed, first clean off the cylinder head to keep foreign matter from falling into the cylinder. Remove the spark plug. Clean and regap it or replace with a new one as recommended by the manufacturer. Pump a couple of squirts of oil into the cylinder and pull the starter cord a couple of times to lubricate the cylinder walls. Replace the spark plug.*

- *Air-cleaner elements are most commonly made of polyurethane or sponge rubber. Wash the element in liquid detergent and warm water, thoroughly dry it (avoid twisting, which could cause it to tear), and saturate it with oil. The easiest way to resaturate with oil is to put the sponge and oil inside a plastic sandwich bag (keeps your hands clean). Also, some engines have paper air filters—these should be removed and replaced each year. Squeeze the excess oil out of the element and reassemble the air cleaner.*

- *Since rotary mowers are subjected to a great deal of vibration that may cause parts to loosen, check and tighten all cap screws, bolts, screws, and nuts. Also check the wheels and tighten or lubricate as needed.*

- *Refill the crankcase with the recommended oil to its proper level. (Some mowers require the oil to be mixed with gas, so read your owner's manual carefully.) Don't overfill the crankcase because engine damage or starting difficulty could result. Lubricate and grease other parts of your mower as recommended in the operator's manual.*

- *Clean all rusty spots and touch up with a rust-inhibiting paint. Cover the mower to protect it from dust and dirt, and store it in a clean, dry place.*

These few easy winterizing techniques will ensure a quick and safe start next spring. If this seems easier said than done, don't be afraid to let your fingers do the walking and call a repair technician. Caring for a lawn mower before putting it away contributes to the reliability and longevity of the machine and helps prevent expensive maintenance later.

Beat the spring rush. Before you put your mower away, take it to your dealer for any servicing you can't do, as well as blade sharpening.

Fall

Fall Care for Water Gardens

Like all garden plants, water-garden plants must be winterized. The annuals (and tropical flowering plants grown as annuals, such as water hyacinths) should be thrown in the compost pile. Perennials can be overwintered. Here's what they need.

Water lilies: Remove the water lilies from the pond and from their containers. Gently wash away all soil and any gravel. Bury the water lilies in a pot of moist sand, cover them, and store in a cool location. Check regularly, adding small amounts of water if necessary. Don't allow them to freeze.

Hardy bog plants such as water iris: Most can stay in the pond all year. Just move them, and their containers, to the deepest part of the water garden. The surface of the soil should be covered with about 12 inches of water. They will freeze solid in cold climates.

Tropical nonflowering plants: This includes umbrella palm, taro, alligator flag, and cannas. These make excellent houseplants as long as you keep them moist at all times. They need lots of sunshine and should be divided before you bring them in.

Once you've taken care of all the plants, it will help save time next year if you drain the pond. Then clean.

And what about the fish? Fish can be left in the pond if it doesn't freeze solid and you have circulating water. If the fish stay, keep the fall debris out of the water. Gases from the decaying debris can be toxic to fish. The fish can also be overwintered in a child's pool or even a trash can filled with water and kept in the basement. The water will need aeration from a small pump. And remember, the cooler the water temperature, the slower the fish will move and the less they'll eat.

At this time of the year you can decide to remove the pump, clean it, and store it in a dry place until spring or leave it running during the winter season.

Fall

Fall

Projects

CLEANING TOOLS

Dirty tools are a sign of a serious gardener. Or just a lazy one. OK, I admit it. After I have been working hard in the garden, my tools look like they've been through the garden wars. But there's a reason behind my lazy madness. I usually have sweat dripping from my brow, dirt crammed under my nails, and an appetite fit for a horse. The last thing I want to do is take more time to clean my tools. It's too much work! I wait . . . and wait . . . and because of my neglect, I've lost many good tools. But I'm changing. Now I try to make it a habit to recondition my tools as soon as the digging season is over. It's a great rainy day project. Here's what to do:

Gather up all your tools and wash them off. In my case scraping them down is more like it! The goal is to remove all the crud, soil, grass, debris, whatever. It might be necessary to scrape off the caked-on mud with steel wool or a stiff brush. If your tools have rust (and mine never do—ha, ha!) rub it off with fine-grade sandpaper. Then with a soft rag, rub oil onto the blade. This will help prevent rust from forming.

If any wooden handles are rough or worn, sand them down. Then rub in some oil. This prevents the wood from drying and cracking during winter. And if you won't be using your tools through the winter, the best place to keep them is in a dry, cool basement.

> *Many chemicals and oils used for cleaning tools are a fire hazard. Read directions carefully and properly dispose of any rags. (Keeping them in water will prevent spontaneous combustion.)*

Here's another tip that will save you a lot of time in the long run. Fill a small bucket (at least 8 to 10 inches deep) with sand. Pour in a quart of either used or new motor oil. Mix the two together. Keep the sand near your tools. After a busy day in the dirt, simply push the tool blade down into the sand and then pull it up and down a few times. The sand acts as sandpaper, removing dirt and debris, while the oil lubricates the blade. Wipe off the excess and you're done. Your tools will last a lifetime . . . as long as you don't lose them!

SUNFLOWER WREATH

Sunflowers are smiling icons in the fall garden. Their huge heads follow the sun until the seed-laden face forces the head into hiding. It droops under its own weight. That's the sign that harvest is soon upon us.

Many people grow the large-headed sunflowers for the tasty by-product, the seeds. But if you'd rather make the warmth of the sunflower last a long time, then you'll enjoy this wreath project.

Supplies for a sunflower wreath:

- *green sunflower head—the bigger the better (from your garden or florist)*
- *straw wreath, slightly larger than the sunflower head*
- *long floral pins*
- *floral adhesive or a hot-glue gun*
- *lemon leaves or something similar*
- *dried flowers or materials for decorating wreath (wheat, milo)*

Attach the edges of the sunflower to the straw wreath. Secure the two together with floral pins by pushing the pins through the flower and into the wreath. With a glue gun or floral adhesive, add lemon leaves around the outside of the wreath. Overlay the leaves. Add some dried or fresh flowers with the glue gun. You might also want to tuck in some wheat and milo. Continue adding and creating until you have the desired look. Hang inside or out in a sheltered location. But remember, if it's outside the birds will take a liking to this wreath.

DECORATING WITH GRAPEVINE

Supplies for grapevine decorations:

- *grapevine*
- *tub of water*
- *floral wire, pipe cleaners, or wax string*

- *dried flowers or other decorative materials (seed pods, acorns, pinecones, small branches, bark from fallen trees)*
- *hot-glue gun*
- *coat hanger wire*
- *tape*

You may not realize it, but decorating your home can be as easy as stepping into your own backyard. There are all kinds of hidden treasures just waiting to adorn your home. The trick is being able to turn sticks and stones into pieces of art. Not an easy task. But I've found that if you start out with a simple idea, you can eventually fine-tune it into a creative masterpiece that you can call your own. A friendly florist showed me how to make some spectacular pieces with grapevine.

Grapevine can be bought in most craft stores or can be picked from wild or cultivated vines. The best time to harvest the vine is in the fall after the foliage has died. The vine will be fairly brittle. To soften and make it more pliable, sink it into a tub of water and let it soak for at least three hours. If you're making a wreath, a round tub will help shape the vine. After the soak, drain the vine. Now it's ready to shape. To maintain the shape, secure the vine with floral wire, pipe cleaners, or wax string.

The next step is deciding what will go on the wreath: dried flowers, dried fruit, or items from the yard. Fresh flowers can be used and allowed to dry right on the grapevine. Some sort of greenery helps to make a nice foundation for the wreath. Attach the objects with a hot-glue gun. Start with the greenery. Clustering the greenery in groups helps to balance the form. You can add as much as you'd like. Then begin layering the flowers and nature bits. Keep adding until you achieve the look you like.

Wreaths are not the only things grapevines can be used for. Winding grapevine around doorways and windows creates a beautiful natural arch. The shape can be established and maintained by using wire from coat hangers and taping it together. Now attach the grapevine. Again, with your hot-glue gun you can attach ornaments to add color and interest.

Grapevine stuffed above kitchen cabinets also brings a nice natural touch to a room. In my home I added dried pomegranates, seeded eucalyptus, pepperberries, and a combination of dried fruits. As the seasons come and go, I'll add different flowers, leaves, or pinecones. It's always changing and always the center of conversation.

Once you get the hang of grapevine, try weaving your own baskets. Or wind it up to create a large ball. During the holidays stuff tiny white lights into the ball and hang in a corner of a room or entrance. They're terrific hanging from tree branches outside!

> *To preserve your decorated wreaths or arches, reach for the hair spray. A light spray will keep the flowers from flaking and help maintain their color while keeping your masterpiece in place.*

HERBAL MUSTARD

A handful of herbs can change plain Dijon mustard into an herbal delight. Here's how:

Select herbs. I like a combination of basil and chives, about ¼ to ⅓ cup. Chop herbs finely. Add to 1 cup of Dijon mustard. Stir in 1¼ tablespoons of white wine. Pour into a decorative jar and wrap with raffia. Store in the refrigerator. Herbal mustards will liven up any sandwich. They make a great baste for chicken, meat, and fish, also a fabulous base for vinaigrette dressing. The mustard will last up to three months.

> *If you don't have fresh herbs, mix 1 tablespoon of dried herbs into the wine. Let sit for 20 minutes to soften herbs before using.*

HERBAL VINEGAR

Go through any gourmet section of the grocery store and you'll see shelves lined with bottles of beautiful herbal vinegars. Sometimes the bottle looks so good, you hate to open it up.

I've been making herbal vinegar for years. When you do it yourself, you won't believe how easy it is and how tasty it can be. This is just one recipe. Once you get the knack of this one, just go out and explore the herb garden. You'll be surprised with the great taste combinations you come up with.

I prefer to use a plain white vinegar. But you can experiment with others for a different flavor and color. Just be aware that apple cider vinegar competes with the herbs' flavor. Here are my simple instructions.

Supplies for chive blossom vinegar:

- *fresh chive blossoms*
- *white vinegar*
- *garlic*
- *tricolored peppercorns*
- *1 quart jar*
- *decorative, tall bottle*
- *scallions (optional)*
- *strainer*

Pick the blooms early in the morning on a dry day. Bring them into the kitchen and set aside.

In a large saucepan heat the vinegar. You want it hot, but not boiling. As the vinegar is heating, stuff the chive blos-

soms into a big jar. Pour the warm vinegar over the top. Almost immediately you'll see the vinegar take on a blush color from the chive blossoms. Seal the jar and let the vinegar cool.

In the meantime, find a decorative tall bottle. Sterilize by dipping in boiling water. Stuff some chive blossoms with their stems attached into the bottle. Add a clove or two of garlic (quartered) and some tricolored peppercorns. A few scallions with a bit of the (washed) roots still attached adds a beautiful and tasteful touch.

After the vinegar has cooled, strain it. Pour the cooled vinegar into the tall bottle. Seal and store. Let the vinegar sit for a few weeks. This allows the vinegar to take on the flavors of the ingredients in the jar.

Purple sage and purple basil turn the vinegar a soft blush color while enhancing the flavor.

LIVING WREATHS

Another great gift from the garden is a living wreath. This is made with a variety of sedums and hens-and-chickens (sempervivum). This wreath can be hung outside. Just be sure to bring it indoors when the weather gets too cold. It makes a great centerpiece.

Supplies for a living wreath:

- *wire frame*
- *sphagnum moss (soaked so it is moist)*
- *fishing line (20 to 30 test)*
- *slow-release fertilizer*
- *toothpicks*
- *variety of succulent plants (hens-and-chickens work especially well)*

Begin by wrapping the wire frame with the sphagnum moss. Secure the moss to the frame by wrapping with fishing line.

Using a pencil, make a depression in the moss. Add a pinch of slow-release fertilizer. Pull off one of the offsets on the sedum or hens-and-chickens. Remove many of the roots attached to the shoots. Put the tiny plant into the hole and drive a toothpick, broken in half, through it. This will keep the tiny plant tacked into the wreath. The toothpicks will eventually rot away after the plant has taken root.

Continue attaching offsets of varieties around the wreath. Water the wreath either by soaking it in a large tub of water or by laying the wreath down on the lawn and sprinkling it. It will take a year before the plants fill in. Since the plants are succulents, they won't need much water. Just keep an eye on the wreath: If the leaves begin to shrivel, water immediately.

BENEFICIAL BATS AND THEIR HOUSES

If you're tired of getting eaten alive by mosquitoes, the best repellent may not be in a bottle, but tucked away in a cave close to your home. Forget about what you've heard about bats being rabid and deadly. Bad spook movies have propagated myths about one of nature's oldest and most useful mammals. They've been around for over 50 million years yet their importance in our environment is just now being understood. Bats are responsible for pollinating most of the tropical fruits you eat. They help to maintain rain forests by spreading seeds and they're great insect eaters. One brown bat will feast on 500 insects in just one hour! A dozen bats could help clean your backyard of pesky insects. And farmers across the country are building bat houses to help reduce the use of toxic chemicals. (If only the bats would eat weeds too!)

Bats are all around us, but if you can provide a shelter for them you're likely to have fewer problems with insects. Like bird houses, bat houses can be purchased or made. Just be sure you meet these requirements:

- *Don't use chemically treated wood.*
- *In cooler northern climates, paint the bat house a dark color to absorb the sun's warmth. In warmer climates, paint the house white to reflect the warming rays.*

Fall

- *Hang the bat house on the east or southeast side of your house to catch the morning sun.*
- *The house needs to be 10 to 20 feet off the ground.*
- *If there is no water source nearby, provide one.*
- *Be patient. It may take a few years for bats to roost in the house.*

An excellent source on how to build bat houses is *The Bat House Builder's Handbook*, by Merlin D. Tuttle and Donna L. Hensley (Austin: University of Texas Press, 1993). It provides clear instructions on how to build a bat house and has great pictures.

Fall Garden Checklist

- *Aerate lawn.*
- *Cut the grass shorter as temperatures get cooler.*
- *Fertilize lawns with a winterizing fertilizer.*
- *Clean leaves off grass and pile or spread in the gardens.*
- *Cut down perennials as they die back.*
- *Wrap the trunks of young trees.*
- *Keep watering evergreens until the first hard freeze.*
- *Clean fallen fruits from around trees.*
- *Dig up tender summer bulbs.*
- *Plant spring bulbs.*
- *Divide bearded iris.*
- *Mulch roses and perennials for winter with heavier materials.*
- *Divide and plant peonies.*
- *As days grow shorter, stop fertilizing houseplants.*
- *Disconnect hoses and drain before freezing weather.*
- *Start paperwhites in early October for Thanksgiving blooms.*
- *Cover strawberries with straw or marsh hay before temperatures drop into the low teens.*
- *In early November, put Christmas cactus in a room that is very cool at night to ensure blooms for holidays*
- *Service lawn mower, or take to a shop for servicing.*
- *Build a bat house.*

▲ Enjoying the fall harvest
Photo by Doug Beasley, courtesy of Rebecca's Garden Magazine

◄ The smiling icon of the fall garden

Taking a break ►

◄ The real workers—the "Rebecca's Garden" television crew

Photos by Andrew Kessler, courtesy of Hearst-Argyle Television Productions

▲ Busy at work

It's that easy—a ▶
sunflower wreath
Photos by Andrew Kessler, courtesy of
Hearst-Argyle Television Productions

▲ Beating the frost
Photo by Michelle Laurita, courtesy of Rebecca's Garden Magazine

Winter

. . . the sleeping season

As the cold north winds blow, there's something very special about being indoors curled up by the fireplace reading a good gardening book. I love winter. The more snow there is, the happier I am. I appreciate the break. Winter is the season that helps us get all those chores done—the ones we kept putting off for the last six months.

With children, it's a time to get creative. Cabin fever can set in quickly. Then it's time to hit the snow. But I'll admit, there comes a point when even I become weary. By March I want to dig in the dirt. Where I live—Wisconsin—good luck! I'll suffer frostbite long before the trowel will penetrate the soil. So I do the next best thing: I plant indoors.

Indoor Gardens

Gardens are not just for the outdoors, you can have a spectacular garden indoors using houseplants.

A big factor of your houseplant success starts from the beginning. Buy only healthy, robust plants. Inspect each plant for insects, disease, and color. Look closely at the leaves; they should be uniform in size without deformations. Their color should be rich green and not pale or yellowing; also stay away from those with brown-edged leaves. The plant should be dense and compact. Remember, bigger is not necessarily better. Once the foliage has passed the health test, look at the soil. If you can see roots coming out of the top or growing through the bottom, pass on the plant. This is an indication the plant has outgrown its home and is probably stressed.

Once you get the plant home, give it a good long drink of water. You'll probably want to do this in the sink or tub to allow the excess water to drain. Keep the plant in a cooler location at first, and continue to keep the soil more moist than usual for the first few weeks. Mist the plant with water to keep the humidity level up and to replicate the greenhouse environment. And just to be safe, keep the new plant away from your existing plants during the transition period. That way if any problems develop, other houseplants won't be affected. If the plant drops some leaves, don't worry—that's typical after a move. But if a lot of leaves fall, the plant is suffering from severe shock. If that's the case, there's nothing you can do but return the plant for a new one.

After two to three weeks in its new home, the plant is ready to grow. Then water once a week or when the soil is dry 1 inch deep and move it to a location with a good light source. Keep in mind, though, that the light source needs to match the plant's requirements; some plants don't need much light. The new houseplant shouldn't be fertilized during the first three months. After that, less is best. Most houseplants should be fed once every three to six months, while the plant is actively growing. This coincides with late spring, summer, and early fall.

If you are one who thinks you can't grow anything indoors, this list is for you: the top 10 easiest plants to grow indoors. These are plants that will tolerate some mistreatment and lack of light and water.

1. *Pothos—Devil's Ivy*
2. *Philodendron*
3. *Spathyphyllum—Peace lily*
4. *Schefflera—Umbrella plant*
5. *Nephthytis—Arrowhead*

6. *Sansevieria—Snake Plant*
7. *Dracaena marginata—Dragon tree*
8. *Palm seifrizi*
9. *Aglaonema—Chinese evergreen*
10. *Dieffenbachia—Dumb cane (leaves are mildly toxic, not safe around small children and pets)*

Some popular harder-to-grow houseplants include:
Ivy
Ficus
Ferns

HOUSEPLANT DOCTOR

Houseplants have their ailments, but knowing how to diagnose and treat the problem can save your plant from the compost pile. Here are some causes of common ailments that affect houseplants.

Shriveled and dry leaves: If the leaves on your plant are shriveled and dry, you might think the plant needs water. But many times it's too much water causing the problem—the number one killer. Here's how to tell: Examine the roots. If they're brown and mushy, they are rotting from too much water. Roots should be very crisp and light-colored. The cure: Stop watering so often. Moisten the soil but don't saturate it.

Wilting and dropping leaves: Probably underwatering. It's just as deadly. The symptoms start with wilting leaves that turn from yellow to brown and finally fall off. Some of the plants will begin drooping from dehydration. The cure: If the plant is small enough, set it in the sink filled partially with water and let the plant sit for an hour or so. It will absorb lots of water. Then just be more consistent with watering. Most plants like to dry out slightly between waterings. Water it enough to moisten the soil but not saturate it.

Spindly stems: This is a sign that the plant needs more light. It becomes spindly and fades in color as it tries reaching for more light. The cure: Put the plant in a place where it will receive more light.

Brown, dead patches: If the leaves on your plant are developing brown, dead patches (especially a plant in a "sunny" window) it probably got sunburned. The cure: Remove the dying leaves, move the plant to an area with less intense light, and water well.

Brown-tipped leaves: One of the most common problems with houseplants is too much salt in the soil. Salts builds up from continuously fertilizing the plant. The cure: Put the plant under the faucet or in the tub. Completely saturate the soil and allow it to drain completely. Repeat this three or four times. This will leach the salt from the soil. Then back off on the fertilizer. I prefer to use half of the recommended dosage for feeding houseplants.

Stunted leaf growth and weak color: Your plant is having growing problems because it is nutrient deficient. The cure: Plants need fertilizer. Usually an all-purpose fertilizer will do. If the veins show through and have a purplish cast, then the plant needs a fertilizer high in magnesium.

Brownish red spots: This is a sign of rust, a fungus that easily moves from one plant to another. It's not often fatal, but it doesn't look very healthy. Once the leaves get rust, they will remain spotty. The cure: Remove all infected leaves. And to protect the plant's new growth from rust, spray the plant with an appropriate fungicide.

White powdery patches: These are a sign of a fungus called powdery mildew. It first appears on the highest leaves, the oldest ones. Powdery mildew can be caused by insufficient air circulation, poor light, and warm and humid days. The cure: Remove affected leaves and move plant to a spot with better light and better air circulation. Maintain a consistent watering schedule and avoid wetting leaves.

Black powdery patches: This is a sign of sooty mold. It appears on both the tops and bottoms of the leaves. It's caused by sucking pests like aphids, which leave behind a sticky, clear film. It's on this sticky solution that the black mold develops. If not taken care of, the mold blocks the leaf from getting light, which then causes the leaf to turn yellow and eventually fall off. The cure: Remove the yellow leaves. Put the plant in a sink and wash the leaves with a weak solution of soapy water. Rinse with clean water. Try to find out what pest is causing the damage and control the pest.

Small, brown corky spots: Usually a sign of too much water. It's called edema and occurs when plant cells burst from too much liquid. Small scabs appear on the leaf and stem. (But sometimes sucking insects can cause the same damage.) The cure: Remove affected leaves and back off on watering.

Blotches of yellow or white on leaves: The spots are water spots and are very common on fuzzy-leaved plants like African violets. These plants are very finicky about watering. The cure: Water from the bottom up. That means place the pot in a bowl of water and let the plant absorb the water through the roots. Be very careful not to touch the leaves with water.

Dirty plants not only look bad, they're not healthy. A buildup of dust and dirt will actually block light from the pores of the leaves, not allowing them to breathe. Make a routine of cleaning your plants with a wet cloth using mild soapy water. Simply wipe down the leaves. (This is also a good way of getting rid of pests and unwanted insects.) For fuzzy-leafed plants use a soft, dry brush.

REPOTTING

Perking up a houseplant sometimes means nothing more than giving it a new home. It's amazing how many people wonder why their schefflera doesn't look as good as it did years ago when it's still sitting in the same pot they purchased it in. One of the signs that the plant needs repotting is top-heavy growth. Does the pot look too small for the plant? If it does, it's top-heavy. Most well-balanced plants will have two-thirds top growth, one-third container. Your judgment is usually a good indicator.

Another repotting indicator comes from the roots. Are they root bound? That means, are the roots packed tightly at the bottom of the container? Are they growing in circles around the base of the pot or even beginning to grow out of the pot?

Watering will also be a clue to when a plant needs repotting. If you find the plant is consuming a lot of water, there's not enough space to accommodate the amount of roots it has.

If you answered yes to any of the above, your plant needs more room to grow. It's important to repot your plants on a regular basis. Not only will the plant get the extra room, but new soil means new nutrients. Potted plants lose soil nutrients through leaching from repeated watering. It literally washes the nutrients away. Repotting is easy. There is only one rule: Select a pot that is only one size larger (no more than 2 inches bigger) than the pot you currently have.

STEP-BY-STEP: REPOTTING

- *First prepare the plant and soil. One to two hours before the repotting, water the plant thoroughly. Also moisten the new potting soil (this can be done ten minutes before planting).*

- *Gently remove the plant from its container. Trim any dead or mushy roots. Then loosen the roots—sort of spread them out. If the plant is root bound, use pruning shears or a sharp knife to score the sides of the root ball from top to bottom. The slice should be fairly shallow, about ¼ to ½ inch deep. Also make a few slices around the base of the root ball where the roots circle around the bottom of the pot. This will encourage the roots to spread out and become established in their new home.*

- *New soil is a must. The rule? Never use soil from outside. You want a good, fertile potting soil that's been sterilized and is free from soil diseases. Certain plants may require a specific soil, but in most cases general potting soil will do. Fill the new container about one-third full with the new soil. Place the plant into the container. Adjust the soil level if necessary to make sure the top of the root ball is about ½ inch lower than the top of the container. Continue adding soil around the root ball. Use a chopstick or pencil to help push the soil in around the sides. Slowly water the plant while still poking the chopstick down on the sides. This will also help remove any air pockets.*

- *The plant may suffer from mild shock. It's always a good idea to keep the plant out of direct sunlight for a week or two. Keep the soil moist but not wet until the roots are established, about two weeks.*

Here's a quick, temporary fix if you can't repot. Gently remove the top 2 inches of the soil and replace with new potting soil.

Root Pruning

If you don't want to move up to a larger pot when repotting, try root pruning. This technique is used to keep the plants the same size in the same pot. I like to refer to it as root surgery. You can tell if the plant needs some root pruning if it shows the same signs mentioned above under repotting: excessive need for watering, root bound, too much top growth for the size of the container. Root pruning will keep all of these in check.

This project is messy, so consider doing it outside or in the garage. If you do it in the house, line a table or counter with newspaper.

STEP-BY-STEP:
ROOT PRUNING

- *Water the plant one to two hours before you prune.*

- *Gently remove the plant from its container. With a clean sharp knife, slice off about 1 inch of the root ball. Do this around the entire root ball, sides and bottom. Carefully scrape off some of the soil on the top of the root ball as well.*

- *Refill the pot with about 1 to 2 inches of new potting soil. Replace the plant and fill in around root ball with fresh soil. Firm with fingers (or a chopstick) and then water well.*

- *This plant will experience shock. Keep it in a cool location with*

*partial sunlight—no direct sun—
for two weeks. Keep the soil moist
but not wet. Eventually, the plant
will bounce right back and maintain its shape and size. Root pruning is a great way to keep your
plants in check.*

*If you want a more compact and dense
plant, simply pinch off the growing tips
of the plants during its growing season.
Pinching forces energy to the side shoots,
making the plant bushier.*

STEM CUTTINGS FOR PLANT CLONING

A great way to duplicate an existing plant is to snip a sample and let it root. One easy way of doing this is a technique called stem cutting. Cut a stem at least 6 to 8 inches long from the plant you'd like to duplicate. Remove all the leaves from the lower 2 to 3 inches of the stem (if left on, the leaves will rot in the water). Submerge the stem up to the remaining leaves in a container of water. Sit back and wait. Within weeks you should begin to see roots growing from the stem. Allow the plant to grow a few roots, but don't wait too long. The longer the roots sit in water, the harder it will be for them to adjust to the soil. Pot up the

rooted cutting and within weeks you'll have another plant at no additional expense.

STARTING SEEDS INDOORS

For the die-hard gardeners, there's nothing quite as fulfilling as starting plants from seeds. And those who've done it know that to be successful requires a lot of baby-sitting. Besides just being fun and sometimes challenging, starting your own plants from seeds allows you to grow a variety of plants not found in local garden centers.

Growing seeds means starting early. Seeds should be ordered by January so you can be ready to plant by February. And be certain to pick seeds appropriate for your zone.

Containers and a growing medium are the next considerations. First the containers. You can use just about anything as long as it's about 2 inches deep and has drainage holes. There are plenty of options around your house. Recycled margarine containers work great. So do clear plastic deli cartons with lids. Just be sure to sterilize the containers by washing with a solution of one part liquid chlorine bleach to nine parts water.

You'll have to spend money on soil that's not really "soil" at all. You need a soil-less growing medium. Potting soil is too heavy for young seedlings and will suffocate them. You can buy premixed soil-less products or make your own using equal parts peat moss and vermiculite or perlite.

Fill the container with the growing medium (it helps if it's premoistened), up to about ¼ inch from the top. Plant the seeds according to the directions. To prevent damping-off, a fungus that kills new seedlings, crumble some dried sphagnum moss over the seed bed. The moss helps suppress pathogens. Keep the soil moist for about seven to fourteen days, until the seeds germinate. Plastic bags or plastic dome covers will ensure a moist environment, but these must be removed as soon as the plant appears, or if the soil becomes moldy or too wet. The seedlings will need lots of light. Grow-lights or fluorescent shop lights are an excellent substitute for the sun. They should be hung as close to the plants as possible without touching. Start with 24 hours of light. As soon as the seedlings emerge cut the light back to 14 to 16 hours a day. As the plants grow raise the lights, keeping them about 3 to 6 inches above the plant. Water the plants as soon as the soil-less mix starts to dry out.

The seedlings have enough stored food to grow first leaves. It's not until the second set, or the true leaves, appears that the seedling has exhausted its food supply and will need to be fed. Water-soluble fertilizers are the best food. Read the directions and then cut the amount of fertilizer down by one-quarter to one-half. If the fertilizer is too strong, it will burn the tender young roots of the seedlings. Transplant seedlings into larger containers if they outgrow their home.

Easy Plants to Start from Seed

Vegetables include eggplants, peppers, broccoli, cauliflower, and tomatoes. Annuals include dianthus, zinnias, marigold, snapdragon, China aster, annual phlox, sweet alyssum, and ageratum.

CACTI

For those of you who would like to have plants but simply don't have the time, cacti are the way to go. With minimal effort, you can have a beautiful arrangement that requires nothing more than sunlight and watering once a month. Here's how you do it:

Select a container, one with good drainage. I like the clay pots; they seem to suit cacti wonderfully. Cover the drainage holes with shards of pottery or screening. This will keep the soil mixture from seeping out. Fill the bottom of the pot with charcoal (you can pick it up at the garden centers). Charcoal acts as a buffer to absorb any excess mineral buildup. Next add the soil. It's important not to use garden soil or ordinary potting soil. You want a mixture with a lot of sand. Garden centers usually carry mixes specifically made for cacti. Add the soil to ½ inch below the rim of the pot. Now you can plant. Add a collection of cacti. To get really creative, add small sticks or stones to help imitate a natural setting. When you're finished, top off with small pea gravel. Water infrequently and fertilize only in the spring and summer.

GROW PALMS EVEN IF YOU DON'T LIVE IN THE TROPICS

The travels of *Rebecca's Garden* took me and the crew to the Fairchild Tropical Garden in Miami, Florida. It's home to one of the largest collections of palms—over 600 varieties. Some grow only 12 inches high, while others shoot 100 feet into the sky. The different shapes are amazing. Some look like concrete pillars from the temples at Karnak in Egypt, growing next to palms that look like living petticoats. It was an awesome sight for someone like me who lives in a northern climate and sees more ice sculptures than palms. But as I learned, you can grow these majestic tropical beauties even if you don't live in the right kind of climate.

Most garden centers carry a few palms. Before you take the plant to the checkout counter, make sure you examine it thoroughly. Look for insect damage or insects themselves. Use some common sense. If the plant looks healthy, it probably is. Once you get the plant home it may shoot up, sometimes outgrowing its pot. Repotting is quite simple. And with palms you can break the repotting rule—pick a pot of any size as long as it's larger. The palm will need it to expand. The container also must have good drainage. To ensure drainage add shards of pottery in the bottom of the container before adding regular potting soil. Remove the palm from its container. The roots should be creamy white. Pop it into the soil and finish filling it up.

There's no pat formula for watering except if it feels dry, water it. But remember, just because they're tropical, it doesn't mean they like sitting in a bog. During the growing season fertilize with an all-purpose fertilizer about once a month. And what about the sun? Most would assume tropical plants thrive in the sunshine. But most smaller palms are considered understory plants, which means they grow under the canopy of much larger plants. So don't get carried away with bright, direct sunlight. Most palms will do just fine near a window with southern exposure.

POPULAR POINSETTIAS

The most popular plant worldwide is not the petunia or begonia but the poinsettia. Every year poinsettias are the top seller in the flower business. But where are the flowers? you ask. Look closely and you'll see the small flowers at the center. They look like tiny colored nubs. Surrounding these are brightly colored leaves; it's really these leaves that attract people.

Select plants with green foliage all the way down to the soil line. If there's any sign of insect damage or disease, select

Winter

another plant. Plants that have small central flowers and bright foliage will perform best.

Poinsettias grow best in rooms that have bright indirect light. Keep them away from drafts or heat. Water the plant thoroughly and allow it to drain. Poinsettias don't like sitting in water. For the best color, keep the plant in a room with temperatures between 65° and 70°F.

After the holidays when the leaves fade to muddy green, cut the plant back to 8 inches high. Treat as you would any other houseplant. Fertilize every three to four weeks and repot when needed. As soon as temperatures warm in the spring, the poinsettia can be moved outdoors, as long as nighttime temperatures are above 50°F.

If you want a fiery array of color next year, bring the plant indoors around October 1 (or when nighttime temperatures drop below 50°F). Give the plant only 6 to 8 hours of light a day, then move it into a dark closet for 12 to 14 hours each night. Keep the temperature between 60° and 70°F.

To set the record straight, poinsettias are not poisonous. It was believed that poinsettias were fatal if ingested. Research from Ohio State University has proven otherwise. Their tests showed no toxicity even if a 50-pound child ate over 500 bracts or leaves. For some people the leaves can irritate the mouth and stomach, sometimes resulting in diarrhea or vomiting. The milky sap may also cause a poison ivy-like blistering if it contacts skin, unless immediately washed off. Yes, it's an irritant, but it won't kill you.

POISONOUS HOLIDAY PLANTS

With the holidays comes a wide array of festive plants and blooming flowers. While many of these decorate our homes as beautiful centerpieces and traditional focal points, they don't taste as good as they look. Some can even be quite toxic.

Holly: Eating the bright, red berries of this plant can cause nausea, vomiting, abdominal pain, and diarrhea.

Jequirity Bean/Indian Prayer Bean: This black-tipped, scarlet bean is used in many dried arrangements. The seeds are poisonous if eaten and can cause death.

Jerusalem Cherry: Every part of this plant contains toxic substances. Eating the fruits or foliage will hurt the heart.

Mistletoe: This is a plant you won't want to kiss. Eating the berries causes acute stomach and intestinal problems.

Toxic Houseplants

After the holidays and throughout the rest of the year, don't forget that some of your other beauties are toxic. Be aware of the potential danger of these common houseplants and flowers:

Amaryllis	*Gladiolus*
Azalea	*Hyacinth*
Bird-of-paradise	*Hydrangea*
Caladium	*Lily-of-the-valley*
Clematis	*Peony*
Crocus	*Periwinkle*
Delphinium	*Stinkweed*

Yew: This evergreen's leaves, seeds, bark, twigs, and berries can be toxic, causing breathing difficulties, uncontrollable trembling, and vomiting if consumed.

Both children and household pets seem fascinated by the bright berries and shiny leaves found on many of these holiday plants and often are tempted to take a bite. Take great care to place your plants and decorations out of reach to both curious fingers and nibbling snouts.

In general, symptoms for plant poisoning can range from rashes to nausea, vomiting to diarrhea. If you suspect that a child has come into contact with any toxic plants, immediately follow these steps:

Mouth: Remove everything from the mouth cavity and carefully wipe the insides with a damp cloth. Carefully look for any swelling or discoloration. If possible, administer one glass of water. Immediately call your local poison control center for further treatment.

Skin: Wash affected area well with soap and water. Immediately call your local poison control center for further treatment.

Eyes: First wash your hands thoroughly with soap and water. Rinse eye with lukewarm water for 10 to 15 minutes. Immediately call your local poison control center for further treatment.

Buying

Christmas Trees

Selling Christmas trees is a big business, so buyer beware—some sellers are going to do everything they can to get a sale. Right down to spraying the tree with green paint to make it look fresher than it really is! So the first piece of advice is to buy from a reputable dealer or cut your own from a local farm.

TYPES OF TREES

It takes eight to ten years for most trees to grow large enough to be Christmas trees. That's a long time for such a short commitment. When we think of the classic Christmas tree, we picture the balsam fir. It's a great tree to put up after the Thanksgiving feast because it keeps fresh longer than the rest. It has a great aroma and holds its needles well. Balsam trees are mainly found in the northern United States. Another popular tree for the holidays is the pine. Long needles are one of the characteristics of pine trees. Pine trees have good needle retention but will not support heavy ornaments. That's something to think about if you plan to decorate with antique ornaments. The Virginia pine is nice for southern climates and the Scotch pine is popular for the Midwest.

Spruce trees are another common holiday gift holder. They are very compact and stiff and have the muscle to hold Grandma's old ornaments. Spruce are usually very nicely shaped, too. The only drawback is that they have a hard time holding on to their needles. So if you set a spruce up too early, you'll have to get the vacuum out. Setting up just a week or two before Christmas will help keep the needles off the floor.

PICKING THE PERFECT TREE

Before heading to the garden center or tree farm, you need to know how tall your ceiling is. Then figure out how much space the tree holder will take. Subtract that from the height of your ceiling. And take off another 6 to 8 inches to leave room for the star on the top! When you find a tree you like that's the right height, look carefully around the entire tree. Any holes or missing branches? How about that hidden trunk? Are there any crazy kinks that will make the tree lean or fall over? (I speak from experience on this one!) And give the tree a good shake. If the needles fly, the tree

is too dry—find another one. Or you can gently tug on the needles. If no needles come off, it's a fresh tree.

Once you get the tree home, it's very important to cut ½ inch from the bottom of the trunk. This will open the pipeline to allow the tree to take up water. The first day, the tree will soak up about a gallon of water. So sink the tree into a large bucket of warm water for the first twenty-four hours. After that the tree will need about 2 to 3 quarts of water a day. Don't let the tree go dry. Just one missed watering will force the tree to create a scab where it was cut at the base. The scab seals the tree and prevents the uptake of water. Once the tree is up, keep it out of the heat and away from fireplaces. The cooler the spot, the longer the tree will last.

When the party is over, toss the tree into the backyard. It will become a great shelter for birds and small animals. And in the spring, use a chipper to turn the branches into mulch for your garden and landscape.

If you get sap from the trees on your skin, it can be easily removed with rubbing alcohol.

Winter

▼ Madison and Taylor testing the soil

▲ Enjoying the fall color
in Minnesota

Madison and Taylor having fun ▼

▲ On the road with Mom

▼ Then there were five . . .

. . . now there are six ▼

◄ Christmas cache

"I want my own book, my ▶
own TV show, my own
magazine . . ."

◀ Before we got our hands dirty

A "friend"ly defeat ▶

◀ Doing what the Goodsells do best—camping

▲ Gardening through the generations ▶
Photo (above) by Nicholsons' of Racine, Inc.

Winter Projects

IVY TOPIARY

Topiaries are not just for the gardeners living on an estate. You can have your own in less than an hour, or at least get it started in that amount of time. The art of forming these plants into ornamental shapes has become a fun part of gardening and accessorizing the home. And it's very easy to do yourself.

The materials can be found at some floral shops and most craft stores.

Supplies for an ivy topiary:

- *wire form*
- *covered wire*
- *ivy plants*
- *decorative pot*
- *wire cutters*

Wire forms come large and small, in the traditional cone, ball, and pyramid shapes, and in not-so-traditional shapes. It's all a matter of taste and creativity. Use covered wire to help train and shape the ivy to cling to the wire form. It's best to start off with a small-leaved variety of

POTTING
SOIL

POTTING
SOIL

Winter

English ivy such as 'Needlepoint.' If your budget allows, spend the extra money to get a larger plant, one with longer stems. This will make it easier to train on the wire frame. Buy a nice, decorative pot into which you can place the potted ivy, or transplant the ivy directly into the pot. Again, it's your call on what to purchase. The pot should be slightly larger than the container the ivy is growing in. The only requirement is drainage holes. If the container doesn't have any drainage holes, either select another pot or drill holes.

Plant your ivy in a good potting soil in the center of the container. Gently place the wire form in the center and push down into the soil until the form is secure. Pick up one of the longer ivy stems and start wrapping it upwards around the wire form, starting at the base. When you reach the sculpture (for example, the wire ball), gently twist the ivy around the form, securing it with small precut pieces of covered wire. Be sure to keep the wire fairly loose around the stem of the ivy; you don't want to girdle the stems. And it's important not to wind the entire ivy stem. Leave a couple of inches hanging. Once the stem is secure, cut off the hanging excess. Don't worry—this doesn't hurt the plant, it helps it. It will encourage new growth on the lower parts of the stems and help the plant get bushier. Repeat the process with the other ivy stems. Just be sure to leave some to drape over the sides of the pot. Once completed, remove one-third of the leaves wrapped around the wire stem. Eventually all will be removed, but too much picking and eliminating will send the plant into shock. Every couple of weeks remove more leaves until you have nothing but a "trunk." Now the key is to sit back and be patient. It takes months, but eventually your new topiary will take on that living sculpture look.

Taking care of your topiary is a breeze. Water regularly to keep it moist but not wet, and fertilize every month while it's actively growing (March through October). Keep it in bright light but out of direct sunlight. Feel free to take it out onto a shady deck during the growing season.

SEED TAPE

I f the kids haven't driven you crazy with cabin fever yet, just wait. They eventually will. So it's important to stay ahead of the game. Be armed and ready to combat cabin fever with fun projects. Here's one that requires few supplies. It's easy and it will be a big help in your backyard garden when spring arrives.

You've probably seen seed tape in garden centers. It's just a roll of paper with seeds glued onto it. It's a simple but ingenious idea, one that can be easily duplicated for a fraction of the cost. Here's how:

Supplies for seed tape:
- *flour*
- *food coloring*
- *roll of heavy-duty paper towels*
- *seeds (radish, lettuce, carrot)*
- *medicine dropper*
- *large plastic bags*
- *plant markers (optional)*

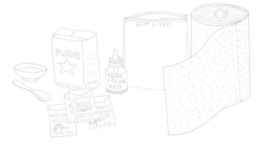

In a small bowl, mix flour and water to create a paste about the consistency of pancake batter. Add a couple of drops of food coloring so the paste is easier to spot on the paper towel. Roll out a few squares of the paper towel. With a medicine dropper space the dots of paste according to the directions on the back of the seed packet. Drop a seed in each dot and let dry.

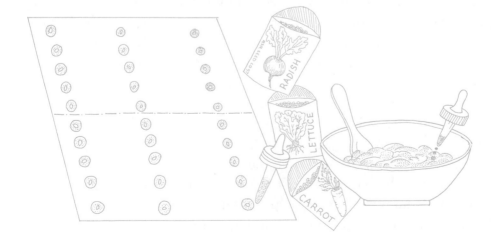

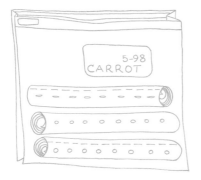

Carefully roll the paper up and store in a large sealed plastic bag. Be sure to insert a label or the seed packet so you don't get your flowers or vegetables mixed up.

When it's time for planting, just unroll the homemade seed tape in the garden, cover with soil, and you're done. No misplaced seeds, no crowding, perfect rows every time. It's simple—and a great project for kids.

GROW YOUR OWN SPROUTS

Who needs an outdoor garden when all you really need is some seeds, a few jars, and a little effort? Your reward will be deliciously crunchy, nutritious sprouts ready to spruce up any sandwich, pasta, or salad. You've probably seen sprouts in the produce department of your local market. By growing your own, however, you can have a variety of sprouts never seen at the grocer's. It's easy and fun, and since seeds sprout quickly, it makes a great indoor project for the kids. Store grown sprouts in the refrigerator to keep fresh.

Here's how:

Supplies for sprouts:

- *wide-mouthed glass jar at least 6 inches deep*
- *seeds: alfalfa, adzuki beans, lentils, chives, chickpeas, mung beans, etc. (Check your local food co-op for more options.)*
- *panty hose or cheesecloth*
- *rubber bands*

Sterilize the container by dipping it in boiling water. Add enough seeds to loosely cover the bottom of the jar. Then add enough warm water to completely cover the seeds, plus 2 inches. Let the seeds soak overnight. This softens their seed coats to speed germination. The good seeds will sink to the bottom while the duds will stay afloat. Remove the duds.

Cover the mouth of the jar with cheesecloth or panty hose and secure with a rubber band. Rinse and drain the seeds, with the cover on, two to three times a day. To prevent mold, be sure to drain well. Place the container in a cupboard. Within three days the smaller seeds will start germinating. Most sprouts are ready to be eaten when they're about ½ inch long, depending on the type of seed and the taste. Pop a few in your mouth. You'll notice that the taste of the sprouts changes as the seeds grow. Put alfalfa sprouts in a sunny spot for a couple of hours if you want them to turn green.

Plants for Stone Paths

To soften the edges or add another dimension to your walkway/patio, plant low-growing plants around the stones. Make sure you know the sun, soil, and water requirements of the plants before you buy, so they will thrive. But the bottom line is to just pack them in, because all you really need is room for your feet. Good plants include:

PLANT	ZONES	HEIGHT
Creeping thyme—nice flowers, aromatic leaves	5–9	1–3 in.
Woolly thyme—silver, hairy-looking leaves	5–9	1–3 in.
Chamomile (Roman)—tiny daisylike flowers; soft feathery slivers of green foliage; can be invasive; best around outer edges of paths	4–8	4–12 in.
Sweet alyssum—cascades over the sides to add a soft look; flowers smell nice; white varieties planted around the outer edges of a garden path will light up the walkway at night	1–11	3–6 in.
Sedum—does well in the sun and even some shade; doesn't need much water	3–9	2 in.
Cinquefoil (potentilla)—blooms spring/summer in full sun	3–10	2–12 in.
European wild ginger—shade plant; blooms in spring	5–9	4–8 in.
Common periwinkle (vinca minor)— shade plant	5–8	4–8 in.
Dalmatian Cranesbill—taller in the shade	4–8	4–6 in.

MAKING YOUR OWN STEPPING STONES

There's something very intimate, very alluring, and very inviting when one comes upon a garden path. Like a magnet it pulls you. That's what a good garden path does—it sparks your curiosity for a garden adventure.

Garden paths can be nothing more than a mown strip of grass, a layer of thick mulch, or the classic—stoned paths wrapped in a dense mound of aromatic groundcover, which releases a beautiful fragrance when crushed by the foot. It's all a matter of choice.

Making paths can be inexpensive or they can break the bank. Natural stone can be costly, yet plain grass paths seem to take away the romance. And concrete stepping stones, found in just about every garden center, are just downright plain and boring. So what's the answer? Why not make your own? It's simple, very inexpensive, and you can design a stone that no one else in the world has. You may not be able to lay the stepping stones until spring, but this is a great indoor activity for the winter. Here's how:

Supplies for stepping stones:

- *mold: deep-dish pizza pan, round or square cake pans, anything that is at least 2 inches deep with straight sides (unlike the sloped sides of a pie tin).*

- *nonstick cooking spray, vegetable oil, or petroleum jelly*

- *concrete mix*

- *water*

- *trowel for mixing*

- *articles for impressions: flowers, stems, tile, glass, etc.*

- *dust mask*

- *newspaper to cover working area*

- *mortar dye*

First you need a mold. To start, try a round cake tin. Spray the tin with non-stick cooking spray or coat with oil.

In a large bucket carefully and slowly pour in about three inches of concrete mix. (Wear a mask to prevent inhalation of the dust, which is bad for your nose and lungs). Slowly pour water into the concrete, mixing constantly. Add water until the mixture looks like cookie dough.

Pour the mixture into the greased cake tin. Press it in around the edges. Pick up the tin and gently tap the bottom on top of your working area to help release any air bubbles.

If you want a plain stepping stone, you're done. But if you want one with personality, now is the time to add it. Try pressing some flowers face down into the concrete. Or be creative with pieces of tile, broken stoneware, or china. Leaves with textured surfaces, like junipers or ferns, also work well. Whatever you use, gently press it into the concrete. Let the stepping stone dry.

Typically, the concrete will set after about two to four hours, but I like to leave it in the mold overnight. The next day carefully remove your stepping stone from the mold and carefully pull away the vegetative imprints. If the plant material sticks, carefully brush it away with a wire brush. Or just let Mother Nature remove it through decomposition. (The tile should be left in.) If done correctly, the leaves will make a wonderful imprint. And there you have it, a great easy accent for your garden!

For colored concrete, add mortar dye (a powder you can pick up at a home repair store or hardware store). Mix it in with the dry ingredients, or mix in with water to get a better idea of the color. Remember, the stone will dry lighter than the colored water appears.

Laying Your Stone Path

Measure the depth of the stone, and then add ½ inch. This is how deep the hole where the stone is going should be. Cut out the sod or soil. Add ½ inch of sand on top of the soil and make it smooth and level. Place the stone on top of the sand and adjust until the stone is flush with the surrounding ground. This is very important, as unlevel surfaces create a tripping hazard. If you intend to make a walkway with stones close together, continue adding stones until you get your desired look. If you're laying stones close together, pour sand over the stones and sweep into the crevices. Wet the walkway or patio and allow water to drain. Then add more sand until the sand becomes level with the stone.

DESIGNER POTS FOR KIDS

I love houseplants, and as you can imagine I have a variety of containers filled with greenery scattered throughout the house. Some have cost an arm and a leg, some are older than my teeth, and some aren't really pots at all. I love them all, but my favorite is one given to me by my son, Taylor. It's a one-of-a-kind, hand-painted terracotta pot, a project he labored over while at a neighbor's house. I'll never forget how proud he was when he showed it to me the first time. I was very touched. He couldn't wait to get something planted in it. What fun! He picked out a plant and we planted it together. The pot, now three years old, still houses the same plant. It greets me every morning as it catches rays from the morning sun. I love it and so do the people who see it.

I was so surprised to find out how easy the project was. So if you need a project for the kids, let them design their own pots either for themselves or as gifts for someone else. This one has fun written all over it!

- *acrylic paints*

- *brushes, sponges, potatoes for prints, etc.*

- *terra-cotta pots*

- *shellac finish or polyurethane*

The instructions are easy. Give the kids paints, brushes, and a pot and let them go to town! If you want to get more adventurous, let them try different textures with sponges or cut their own stamps from raw potatoes. They will have a ball. The only rule? You can't interfere, unless of course they decide to paint something other than the pots!

When the pots are done, let them dry thoroughly. You can add a finish by either painting or spraying on shellac. Mine doesn't have a finish and it still looks great.

DESIGNER POTS FOR THE BIG KIDS

If the pot-painting party turns out to be a success for the kids, you may want to try your hands at it. These methods are for a more "grown-up" look.

Distressed decor is hot. What takes nature years to produce can be done in an hour. These techniques will mimic the look of aged pottery and tarnished cop-per. All you need are acrylic paints and a few other supplies. Everything can be picked up at local craft stores.

Crackle Finish

This look requires layering paint so that the top coat crackles, revealing a base coat. Success comes in the color selection. Contrasting colors seem to work best. First-timers may want to use white as the base (the color of the crack) and a darker color for the top.

Supplies for crackle finish:

- *acrylic paint for base coat*

- *acrylic paint in different color for top coat*

- *terra-cotta pot*

- *paintbrush*

- *crackle medium (causes the paint to look crackled)*

- *glaze (acrylic sealer)*

Start by painting the base coat color on the pot. Let the paint dry thoroughly, about half an hour. Brush on a thin layer of crackle medium, being sure to completely cover the pot. Let this dry thoroughly, at least one hour. The medium should be dry to the touch and not tacky.

Next apply the second color for the top coat. This step is a little tricky; it requires you to work quickly while applying the paint smoothly. Carefully add the paint without overlapping strokes (otherwise it will lift the other paint). Cover the entire pot and wait. It takes about an hour for the pot to dry while transforming into a rustic, crackled appearance. The final step is to seal the finish. Apply an acrylic sealer on the outside (and inside if you prefer), let it dry, and you're done!

Patina Finish

Tarnished copper is almost as beautiful as new copper. Getting that look on a pot is easy but may require a few tries to perfect.

Supplies for patina finish:

- *terra-cotta pot*
- *three colors of paints: teal green, dark brown, and mossy yellow-green*
- *2 very small natural sponges*
- *paintbrush*
- *gold wax metallic finish*
- *piece of soft cloth*
- *acrylic sealer (optional)*

Start by painting the entire pot teal green. Let it dry completely.

To achieve the aged look of copper, pour a small amount of the brown and mossy yellow-green paint onto a plate. Dip one sponge in the brown paint. You don't want a lot—once you've dipped it, blot the paint on a scrap piece of paper to remove the excess. Then gently blot the sponge lightly onto the sides of the pot, starting on the bottom. Blot the bottom third, the top edge, and the rim of the pot. Let dry.

Dip a clean damp sponge into the mossy yellow-green paint. Again blot off the excess. Then blot the sponge lightly and randomly over the dark brown paint. You'll quickly see how mixing the two colors gives the pot the look of oxidized copper. Once you're satisfied, add the final touch. Rub the soft cloth into the metallic wax finish and gently rub a small amount onto the pot. Use sparingly as the wax is intended to highlight a few areas without covering the pot. Rubbing around the edges, top, rim, and bottom and in random spots is best for highlights. Let dry.

Once the pot is dry, you can apply acrylic sealer or other sealant to keep the paint from fading. Or leave alone and you're finished.

NEON TOOLS

If you've gardened long enough, then you no doubt have lost a tool or two only to find it the next season buried in with the tubers. It's easy to do since the colors of the handles usually blend right in with the color of the soil or the green foliage. What you need are tools that stand out in the garden. Here's how to get them in two easy steps. This is another great project for kids. And as you'll literally see, these tools may look outrageous, but they'll be next to impossible to lose in the garden.

Supplies for neon tools:

- *a variety of acrylic paints (the hotter the color, the better)*
- *fine-grade sandpaper (for wooden handles)*
- *bucket of sand*
- *brushes*
- *raffia (if giving as gift)*

Thoroughly clean the tool handles. If wood, sand thoroughly to remove the varnish or finish. Let dry completely.

Place the blades of the tools in a bucket of sand to hold the handles upright. Then paint the handles. The brighter the color, the easier they will be to locate. Allow the tools to dry thoroughly.

Great gift idea: When completely dry, tie raffia around the handle and give the gift of gardening to someone you love. They'll never leave another tool in the garden.

Here's a treat any bird is sure to love all year long. Stuff creamy peanut butter in a pine cone. Roll the cone in bird seed. Attach a long string or raffia and hang on the end of a branch.

BATH BAGS

After a long, hard day nothing beats a good long soak in a warm bath. If you want to make it a form of therapy, just add a handful of herbs. It's a great way to pamper yourself. And you can concoct a mixture to alleviate stress or help generate a good mood.

Word to the wise: Find something to hold the herbs. Don't make the mistake I once did early on during my discovery of herbs. I put a handful of herbs directly into the water. I was picking bits and pieces of herbs out of my hair and off my skin for days! A mesh bag works well. Or just buy a couple of yards of cheesecloth; cut out large circles and tie them up around your herbs. A nylon stocking works, too. If you have a large tea ball or one of those containers used for holding the herbs when boiling shrimp, they work well, too. Whatever you use, it must allow water to seep in and out.

The herbs you mix together will be determined by the sensation you want to create.

RELAXER/STRESS
RELIEVER/SLEEP INDUCER

Mix together:

⅓ cup coarse sea salt (great for smoothing the skin)

⅓ cup hops (induces sleep)

⅓ cup chamomile (for relaxation and soothing)

¼ cup lavender

6 rosebuds

Fill the bath bag, tie with string or raffia, and run under hot running water. Then let it steep in the tub while you soak.

Mix together:

⅓ cup peppermint (excellent for lifting spirits)

⅓ cup ginger root (excellent for sore muscles)

⅓ cup rosemary

Small handful calendula flowers

Fill the bath bag, secure the opening, and run under lukewarm water. Then let the bag steep in the tub.

FOR SORE MUSCLES

Mix together:

⅓ cup sage (relaxes muscles)

⅓ cup chamomile (for relaxation and soothing)

Small handful juniper berries

Small handful of fragrant herbs: bay, scented geranium, lavender, or sandalwood

Fill the bag, tie securely, and run under warm running water. Then let it steep in the tub.

TROUGH GARDENS

As the manufacture of cars started booming in the early 1900s, the need for horses diminished. The troughs the horses drank from became useless . . . at least for the horses. Since the watering troughs were made out of stone, they were much too heavy to move. Most sat collecting rain and cobwebs for years until someone had the brilliant idea to use the troughs for a container garden. The idea took off and suddenly the troughs were spilling over not with water but with bouquets of flowers.

Now here it is the '90s, and the trough garden concept is back. Now the real thing is hard to find and expensive. Instead there are nifty ways of making trough gardens that look as old as the originals. Here's how:

Supplies for a trough garden:

- *a form: a large and wide bucket, a wooden crate, or a wooden box*
- *bubble wrap, dry-cleaner bags, or plastic garbage bags*
- *chicken wire*
- *peat moss*
- *perlite*
- *portland cement*
- *throw-away gloves*
- *dust mask*

- *shovel*
- *wheelbarrow*
- *putty knife*

The first step is to get the form ready. Line the inside of the form with plastic bags. Twist and tie knots in the bags to make a gnarly mess—the bumpier the better. This will give the outside of the trough container a rough texture and a natural look. Don't cover the bottom. You want that flat so the container can stand upright.

The next step is to mix the dry ingredients in the wheelbarrow. Mix equal parts of peat moss, perlite, and portland cement. (For one mold, 2 gallons of each should be enough.) Make sure you use a face mask. The fine dust from cement is easy to inhale and bad for the lungs.

Add water slowly and start stirring. The mixture should have the same consistency as cottage cheese. Then, working quickly, press the cement mixture into the mold. Firmly press it into the corners, on the bottom, and around the sides. You are creating a bowl inside the form. When your bowl is three-quarters finished, lay strips of chicken wire along the bottom and the sides. This will reinforce the pot, making it stronger. Cover the chicken wire strips with more cement mixture.

Once the "bowl" is shaped, poke a hole in the bottom for drainage. Allow the pot to sit in the form for three to five days to dry. Then gently remove the form. Remove any sharp edges with a putty knife. To give the trough a natural look, rub some dry portland cement on the exterior. Now take the pot outdoors and let it cure for three to five weeks. Fill with water often to help leach out excess lime. Then you're ready to fill it up. Use a sterilized potting soil or soil-less mix and begin planting.

If you want any stone or concrete structure to look as though it has aged with time, paint it with buttermilk or yogurt. If left in the sun lichens will grow on it; in the shade moss will grow.

Winter Garden Checklist

- *Prune crabapples, apples, pears, and large shade trees.*
- *Use sand on slippery sidewalks instead of chemical de-icers, which can damage your shrubs, trees, and lawns.*
- *Order seeds in January.*
- *In January, remove geraniums from winter storage and repot.*
- *Start slow-growing seeds indoors in February.*
- *Get kids gardening. Have them plant seeds or tops of fruits and vegetables. Try carrot and pineapple tops, an avocado pit, or a potato (sweet and regular).*
- *Remove faded amaryllis flowers. Leave stalk on until it fades.*
- *Don't fertilize houseplants in winter. Wait until you see new growth in early spring.*
- *Remember to sterilize containers used for starting seeds.*
- *Water houseplants with warm water.*
- *Check houseplants regularly for pests or diseases and control with appropriate treatment.*
- *Make seed tape.*
- *Check plant roots to determine whether repotting or root pruning is necessary.*

Vegetables

Asparagus

Site

LIGHT: Full sun (about eight hours of sunlight per day).

SOIL: Rich, well-drained. Amend bed with lots of compost, rotted manure, or other organic material.

SPECIAL NEEDS: Asparagus is a perennial that can live for many years. Carefully select placement before planting. Plant in a separate bed or at the side of the vegetable garden so it won't interfere with rotating crops, rototilling, or digging in vegetable beds. Roots can grow up to 6 feet down, so make sure soil is cultivated deeply and locate plantings away from tree roots.

Planting

WHEN: Plant transplants (crowns) in the spring in colder climates; in warmer climates asparagus can also be planted in the fall.

DEPTH OF SEED: 1½ inches. Most prefer to plant one-year-old nursery-grown crowns because seeds take so long.

DEPTH OF TRANSPLANT: 12 inches deep for one-year-old crowns. Only 2 to 3 inches of soil or compost should be used to cover the roots at this time. A mixture of soil and compost should be used to fill the trench gradually during the growing season.

SPACING: 18 inches between crowns.

YEARS TO MATURITY: 3 years.

SPECIAL NEEDS: Asparagus is planted in well-amended trenches that are at least 12 inches deep and about 1½ feet wide. Make a mound at the bottom of the trench for each crown, using compost or rotted manure. Gently untangle and spread the roots over the top of the mound. Cover the roots completely and the tip of the plant with about 2 inches of soil. Don't completely fill in the trench now. As the spears grow, gradually add more soil.

Growing

WATERING: Needs consistent moisture, especially when spears are growing.

FERTILIZING: Once in early spring and once after harvest.

SPECIAL NEEDS: Stake tall plants to increase garden space.

Harvest

WHEN: None the first year. The second year, take only a few spears. The third year, take as much as you want. Spears are ready when 6 to 8 inches high, usually March through June. (Over 8 inches and they've passed their ideal harvest stage.)

HOW: Using sharp knife, cut at base or simply bend spear until it snaps.

TIPS: Keep harvesting the spears, or the plant will shoot up ferns and end the harvest season. Don't cut plants down until the ferns turn yellow or brown. This allows the maximum amount of nutrients to return down to the roots and ensures a larger crop next year.

Storage

TECHNIQUES: Refrigerate with a damp paper towel around the ends. Excellent for freezing and good for canning. Frozen asparagus should be eaten within six months.

STORAGE LIFE: Eat right away because asparagus doesn't keep long in the refrigerator.

Nutrition

High in vitamins A and C, also potassium.

Pest/Disease Control

Rust disease affects both asparagus and strawberries, so don't grow these crops in the same area. Keeping the garden tidy will help reduce the number of asparagus beetles. Like garlic, asparagus has a strong odor, so it naturally repels most insects.

History/Folklore

This member of the lily family has been cultivated since ancient Egyptian times. Native to the eastern Mediterranean and Asia Minor. It was a thriving crop in the New World in 1672. Asparagus is Greek for "to swell."

Tip

Water heavily in October and November until ground freezes.

Bean, Bush

Site

LIGHT: Full sun.

SOIL: Rich, well drained, and not too acidic.

SPECIAL NEEDS: Keep area free from weeds.

Planting

WHEN: After danger of frost and when soil temperature reaches 60°F.

DEPTH OF SEED: 1½ to 2 inches.

DEPTH OF TRANSPLANT: Not applicable—Seeds are sown directly in garden.

SPACING: 3 to 6 inches depending on variety; space rows 20 inches apart.

DAYS TO MATURITY: Varies with variety from 45 to 100 days. Bush: 45 to 65 days; Pole: 60 to 70 days.

SPECIAL NEEDS: Beans will rot in cold, wet soils.

Growing

WATERING: Water regularly, about 1 inch per week, especially while plant is producing flowers. Drought affects number of beans in pods, causes blossoms to drop, and causes misshapen pods.

FERTILIZING: Not too much. Go light on nitrogen; better to scratch potassium into the soil or a little phosphorus.

SPECIAL NEEDS: Pole types.

Harvest

Plants stop producing beans when the temperature is higher than 80°F. As temperature cools, the beans will grow.

WHEN: Beans are ready when pods are just barely plump, about the thickness of a pencil. The bean should easily snap when bent. If pods become lumpy from seeds inside, you've waited too long. If growing for dried beans, leave pod on plant and harvest when brown and dry.

HOW: Hand-pick from plant.

TIP: If pods are allowed to mature fully on the vine, the plant will stop producing more beans.

Storage

TECHNIQUES: Excellent frozen or dried.

STORAGE LIFE: 1 year dried; 6 to 12 months frozen.

Nutrition

High in protein, amino acids, A and B complex vitamins, iron, calcium, phosphorus, and potassium.

Pest/Disease Control

Weather with high temperatures, high humidity, and heavy rainfall tends to bring on many bean diseases. The best defense is to buy good seeds and rotate the crop annually.

History/Folklore

Beans come in a tremendous variety. They originate from all corners of the world and thrive on vastly different conditions ranging from cool to tropical. Beans are known to have been eaten 5,000 years ago in Asia and 4,000 years ago in Europe, and they were a staple of Native Americans when settlers arrived in the New World.

Tip

Beans help fertilize the soil by releasing nitrogen from the nodules in their roots.

Beet

Site

LIGHT: Sun or partial shade.

SOIL: Tolerates most loose soil, but never clay, compacted, or rocky soil.

SPECIAL NEEDS: All stones should be removed from top 5 inches of the soil to encourage good root growth.

Planting

WHEN: As soon as soil can be worked in spring, or plant middle to late summer for fall crops.

DEPTH OF SEED: $\frac{1}{2}$ to 1 inch deep.

DEPTH OF TRANSPLANT: Doesn't transplant well, so just grow from seeds.

SPACING: 2 inches apart; space rows 12 to 18 inches apart.

DAYS TO MATURITY: 55 to 65 days.

SPECIAL NEEDS: Good idea to soak seeds for 12 hours before planting.

Growing

WATERING: Be consistent. Beets become tough and woody if soil dries out. They also stop growing at the first sign of a dry spell.

FERTILIZING: Quick growth is the key to great beets. Amend soil prior to planting. Scratch a 10-10-10 fertilizer into the soil three weeks after planting.

SPECIAL NEEDS: Seeds contain clusters of plants, which will need to be thinned as beets grow. Thin down to one plant.

Harvest

WHEN: When top beet is about 2 inches wide, usually June through October.

HOW: Gently pull the base of the greens.

TIP: Beet should be a bit larger than a golf ball, about 2 inches in diameter.

Storage

TECHNIQUES: Great for freezing, pickling, and canning.

STORAGE LIFE: 3 months, stored in sand in cellar; 3 weeks in a refrigerator.

Nutrition

Vitamins A and C, also potassium. Greens contain more vitamins than roots and are good sources of iron and calcium.

Pest/Disease Control

Rabbits and groundhogs love eating beet tops. Use a small fence to deter the pests. Flea beetles and aphids can also attack the foliage. Crop rotation will prevent most diseases.

History/Folklore

First beet seeds brought to America in 1806.

Tip

Trouble skinning? Drop beets in boiling water for a few minutes to loosen skins. All parts are edible. Don't throw out the green tops. They're edible and especially good steamed.

Broccoli

Site

LIGHT: Full sun.

SOIL: Rich well-drained, rich in nitrogen and calcium (lime).

SPECIAL NEEDS: Plant very early for a spring crop or later for a fall crop. Broccoli needs cool nights to develop flower heads; it doesn't like hot weather. Once summer temperatures climb above 85°F, broccoli will flower. The buds quickly open and the plant will grow tall and leggy.

Planting

WHEN: Start seeds indoor 5 to 7 weeks before last frost date.

DEPTH OF SEED: $\frac{1}{2}$ inch deep.

DEPTH OF TRANSPLANT: Same depth as in container.

SPACING OF TRANSPLANTS: 2 feet apart (this extra room will allow room for additional side shoots to grow). Rows should be 24 to 30 inches apart.

DAYS TO MATURITY: 60 to 80 days.

SPECIAL NEEDS: Do not rotate where other cabbage-type plants were planted the previous two years, including cauliflower, Brussels sprouts, and cabbage.

Growing

WATERING: Broccoli likes a lot of water. Important to be consistent during the growing cycle. Irregular watering will produce premature heading and miniature heads.

FERTILIZING: Start with well-amended soil. Mix in compost or rotted manure or a handful of 10-10-10 fertilizer.

Harvest

WHEN: Cut when the head is very tight, before buds begin to open.

HOW: Cut head and about 4 inches of stalk with a sharp knife.

TIP: If you can see yellow buds, you've waited too long. It's better to harvest too early than too late.

Storage

TECHNIQUES: Refrigerate in a plastic bag. Freezes well.

STORAGE LIFE: 4 days in refrigerator.

Nutrition

Vitamins A and C, iron, calcium, phosphorus, and potassium.

Pest/Disease Control

Place collars around stems of transplants to prevent cutworm damage. Aphids can be controlled with ladybugs. Rotate every year to prevent disease and insect problems.

History/Folklore

This member of the cabbage family originated in the Mediterranean and Asia Minor about 2,000 years ago.

Tip

Soak fresh broccoli in salty water to draw out any worms tucked in the head.

Brussels Sprouts

Site

LIGHT: Full sun.

SOIL: Dig compost into the area two weeks before planting.

SPECIAL NEEDS: Protect mature plants from heavy winds so they don't bend and break.

Planting

WHEN: Start seeds indoors 6 weeks prior to last frost date.

DEPTH OF SEED: $\frac{1}{2}$ inch deep.

DEPTH OF TRANSPLANT: Same depth as in container.

SPACING: 14 to 18 inches apart. Space rows 24 to 30 inches apart.

DAYS TO MATURITY: 100 days from seeds.

Growing

WATERING: About 1 inch per week.

FERTILIZING: Place a spoonful of 5-10-5 in the hole before planting.

SPECIAL NEEDS: Break off most of the bottom leaves in late summer. In mid-September pinch off the top of plant to encourage growth of sprouts.

Harvest

WHEN: Pick when the size of a golf ball.

HOW: Just twist. Or cut with a knife, being careful not to cut too close to the stem.

TIP: Harvest the lower sprouts first.

Storage

TECHNIQUES: Refrigerate in a plastic bag.

STORAGE LIFE: 3 to 4 days.

Nutrition

Vitamins A and C, calcium, potassium, and iron.

Pest/Disease Control

Collars can prevent cutworm damage.

History/Folklore

Named after the capital of Belgium. Developed in the sixteenth century.

Tip

Before the first hard freeze, the plant can be dug up and transplanted to an indoor container. Make sure to keep the soil damp, and it will continue to produce sprouts. Otherwise allow the plant to get nipped by light frost. This sweetens the sprouts.

Cabbage

Site

LIGHT: Full sun.

SOIL: Fertile and neutral to slightly alkaline (not acidic). Dig in lots of well-rotted manure two weeks before planting.

SPECIAL NEEDS: Prefers cool weather.

Planting

WHEN: Start seeds indoors 6 weeks before last frost date.

DEPTH OF SEED: ½ inch.

DEPTH OF TRANSPLANT: Same depth as in container.

SPACING: 12 inches apart; space rows 2 feet apart.

DAYS TO MATURITY: 90 to 150 days from seeds.

SPECIAL NEEDS: To minimize pest and disease problems, don't plant in same location where any related crops like Brussels sprouts, kale, broccoli, or cauliflower grew in the last two years.

Growing

WATERING: Especially important during head development.

FERTILIZING: Heavy feeders. Enrich soil before planting, and then supply garden fertilizer every 3 to 4 weeks.

Harvest

WHEN: When you're ready to eat it!

HOW: Cut off outer leaves and twist off head.

Storage

TECHNIQUES: Refrigerate in a plastic bag.

STORAGE LIFE: One week.

Nutrition

Vitamins A and C; good source of fiber.

Pest/Disease Control

Sprinkle dill seeds on the leaves, or grow thyme nearby, to discourage bugs. Spreading wood ashes around each plant will discourage maggots.

History/Folklore

Originated in coastal areas of western Europe. The first record of a hardheaded variety was in 1536. Still grows wild in France and England.

Tip

Head will split if left on the plant too long.

Carrot

Site

LIGHT: Full sun or partial shade.

SOIL: Will tolerate most deep, loose soils, but has a hard time in clay or acidic soils. Prefers a sandy loam soil.

SPECIAL NEEDS: Pick a site that is free of rocks and debris to prevent misshapen roots.

Planting

WHEN: Sow outdoors in early spring, as soon as the soil can be worked.

DEPTH OF SEED: Seeds are very small; simply press them into soil.

DEPTH OF TRANSPLANT: Not applicable; doesn't transplant well.

SPACING: 1 to 2 inches apart; space rows 6 inches apart.

DAYS TO MATURITY: 60 to 80 days.

TIP: To assure good germination, keep seedbed moist until seeds sprout.

Growing

WATERING: About 1 inch per week.

FERTILIZING: Add well-rotted (not fresh!) manure or compost to heavy or sandy soils.

SPECIAL NEEDS: Thin out the rows to allow ample growing room, leaving 2 inches between each plant.

TIP: Mound 1 to 2 inches of soil around the tops of carrot root $1\frac{1}{2}$ months after sowing seed to prevent them from turning green.

Harvest

WHEN: As soon as they reach eating size until late fall.

HOW: Grab the green top near the base of the root and pull gently. Works best when soil is wet.

TIP: The darker green the top, the larger the carrot.

Storage

TECHNIQUES: Store covered in moist sand. Keep in cool location.

STORAGE LIFE: 3 months in moist sand; 2 weeks in the refrigerator.

Nutrition

Vitamin A. Strained carrots are used to treat diarrhea in babies.

Pest/Disease Control

Maggots of carrot root flies feed off roots. Harvest the roots as soon as this insect is detected in the patch. Prevent bacterial root rot by rotating the crop annually.

History/Folklore

Fashionable ladies once sported carrot tops on their hats. Herbalists have used them to cure assorted ailments, from gastric disorders to infertility.

Tip

Planting small amounts in 3-week intervals extends the harvest season.

Cauliflower

Site

LIGHT: Full sun to partial shade.

SOIL: Tolerates most soil types as long as nitrogen is supplied.

SPECIAL NEEDS: If soil is acidic, add lime a few weeks before planting.

Planting

WHEN: Start indoors 5 to 7 weeks before last frost date. But don't transplant outdoors until 2 weeks before last frost.

DEPTH OF SEED: $\frac{1}{2}$ inch deep.

DEPTH OF TRANSPLANT: Same depth as in container.

SPACING: 18 inches apart; space rows 30 inches apart.

DAYS TO MATURITY: 70 to 100 days.

Growing

WATERING: Needs plenty of water, especially in hot areas.

FERTILIZING: Should be done on regular basis every 3 to 4 weeks. Use fertilizers high in nitrogen.

SPECIAL NEEDS: Some cauliflower varieties must be blanched to retain their white head color. To blanch, as soon as the heads are 2 inches across, bring leaves up and over the head and tie.

Harvest

WHEN: Pick when the curds are still tightly clustered. If they begin to spread out, you've waited too long.

HOW: With a sharp knife, cut 6 inches of the stem.

TIP: Head will discolor and get loose if left on the plant too long.

Storage

TECHNIQUES: Best frozen or pickled. Can be refrigerated in a plastic bag.

STORAGE LIFE: 5 days in the refrigerator.

Nutrition

Vitamins A and C, also iron.

Pest/Disease Control

Root maggots are sometimes a problem in the fall. In the spring, cover seedlings with row covers to prevent flies from laying eggs.

History/Folklore

Cultivated in the Mediterranean and Asia Minor for more than 2,000 years. Brought to the United States in the 1920s.

Tip

Look for varieties described as self-blanching if you don't want to bother tying leaves over cauliflower heads.

Celery

Site

LIGHT: Full sun.

SOIL: Loose and loamy. Rich in organic matter—compost, manure, etc. The wetter the soil, the better.

SPECIAL NEEDS: Must have rich, fertile soil to produce a good-quality crop. If soil is acidic, add lime at least 2 weeks before planting.

Planting

WHEN: Sow seeds indoors 10 weeks before the last frost.

DEPTH OF SEED: $\frac{1}{4}$ inch deep; use light sand or soil-less mixture.

DEPTH OF TRANSPLANT: As deep as the container.

SPACING: 1 foot apart; space rows 18 inches apart.

DAYS TO MATURITY: 115 to 135 days.

SPECIAL NEEDS: Use mulch around the base of the plants to maintain moisture levels.

TIP: When planting in garden fertilize with liquid fertilizer.

Growing

WATERING: Don't let the soil dry out.

FERTILIZING: With 10-10-10 every 2 to 3 weeks.

SPECIAL NEEDS: Mulching around plant if overnight low temperatures drop below 50°F.

Harvest

WHEN: Any time during the growing season.

HOW: Snap or cut off stalks near the ground.

Storage

TECHNIQUES: Store in plastic bag in refrigerator.

STORAGE LIFE: Two weeks.

Nutrition

Vitamins A and C, sodium, and potassium.

Pest/Disease Control

Thorough weeding should reduce the chance of an aphid infestation.

History/Folklore

Although wild forms were found throughout low-lying European and southern Asian wetlands, celery most likely originated near the Mediterranean. Celery was first used as a medicine. In the 1600s, the French were the first to use it as a food. In the United States, celery was commercially produced in Kalamazoo, Michigan, beginning in 1874.

Tip

If you want light colored stalks you can blanch them. When stalks are 18 inches tall wrap the stalks with paper bags or several layers of newspaper. Leave 6 to 8 inches of tops exposed.

Chard, Swiss

Site

LIGHT: Full sun to part shade.

SOIL: Does well in all soil types. Enrich soil with plenty of organic matter.

SPECIAL NEEDS: Make sure soil is tilled well, roots can grow 6 feet deep.

Planting

WHEN: Sow seeds outdoors as soon as soil can be worked in spring.

DEPTH OF SEED: $\frac{1}{2}$ inch deep.

DEPTH OF TRANSPLANT: No need to transplant, as it's so easy to grow outside.

SPACING: 6 to 10 inches apart; space rows 18 to 24 inches apart.

DAYS TO MATURITY: 55 to 65 days.

SPECIAL NEEDS: Keep plants thinned to get a continual supply of green through the growing season.

Growing

WATERING: Don't let soil dry out.

FERTILIZING: Mix in all-purpose fertilizer prior to planting.

SPECIAL NEEDS: Swiss chard tolerates heat and cold well, though it produces smaller leaves in hot weather.

Harvest

WHEN: Harvest when leaves are large and crinkled.

HOW: Cut leaves down to 2 inches above ground. New leaves will continue to sprout.

TIP: If plants are continually harvested, they will continue to produce leaves.

Storage

TECHNIQUES: Store in a plastic bag in the refrigerator. Freezes well.

STORAGE LIFE: 2 weeks.

Nutrition

Vitamins A and C, potassium, and iron.

Pest/Disease Control

Pests are usually not a major problem.

History/Folklore

Used before Roman times.

Tip

If you harvest most of the leaves at one time, give plants a boost with fish emulsion or other liquid fertilizer to encourage speedy regrowth.

Chives

Site

LIGHT: Full sun.

SOIL: Prefer rich, loose soil. Thrive in a combination of two parts compost, one part sand, and one part garden soil.

Planting

WHEN: When soil can be worked.

DEPTH OF SEED: $\frac{1}{4}$ inch deep.

DEPTH OF TRANSPLANT: Same depth as in container.

SPACING: 8 to 10 inches.

DAYS TO MATURITY: 80 to 90 days.

Growing

WATERING: Water frequently.

FERTILIZING: Fish emulsion works great.

SPECIAL NEEDS: Prevent flowering to encourage more growth.

Harvest

WHEN: Late spring.

HOW: Cut with a scissors.

TIP: Dig out in winter.

Storage

TECHNIQUES: Can be dried or frozen.

STORAGE LIFE: Chives wilt quickly—don't keep long in refrigerator.

Nutrition

High in vitamin A.

History/Folklore

Cultivated in ancient China. Chives were used to chase away evil spirits.

Tip

If the chives set flowers, remove before they set seed. Otherwise your entire garden will become a chive patch.

Corn, Sweet

Site

LIGHT: Full sun.

SOIL: Well-drained; prefers pH 5.8 to 6.5.

SPECIAL NEEDS: Don't crowd plants. Plant corn in blocks 3 to 4 rows wide to ensure pollination and good yields.

Planting

WHEN: After all danger of frost has passed.

DEPTH OF SEED: 1 to 2 inches deep

DEPTH OF TRANSPLANT: Not applicable.

SPACING: 10 to 14 inches apart; space rows 30 to 36 inches apart.

DAYS TO MATURITY: 60 to 90 days.

SPECIAL NEEDS: Corn needs warm temperatures (70° to 80°F) to grow well, so don't rush planting. Soil temperatures should be at least 62°F. Or as some farmers say, plant when oak leaves are as big as squirrel ears.

TIP: Soaking seeds overnight will speed germination.

Growing

WATERING: Must be very consistent with watering, especially when corn is tasseling.

FERTILIZING: Corn is a heavy feeder and likes lots of nitrogen. Mix fertilizer, rotted manure, or compost into the soil prior to planting. Then scratch fertilizer into soil when stalks are 8 to 10 inches, then again when corn tassels develop.

SPECIAL NEEDS: Cultivating is important. By the time the stalks reach knee-high, you should have cultivated around three times.

Harvest

WHEN: When silks turn brown but are still damp.

HOW: Sharply twist the ear from the stalk.

TIP: To test if an ear is ready for picking, squeeze a kernel. If a milky liquid pops out, the ear is ripe.

Storage

TECHNIQUES: Good fresh, frozen, canned, or pickled.

STORAGE LIFE: Best cooked immediately after harvest. If you can't cook immediately, store with husks on in the refrigerator.

Nutrition

Vitamins A and C and protein.

Pest/Disease Control

Common smut causes large, silvery white or sooty black growths on the ears. It usually occurs when plants are 1 to 3 feet tall, and when weather is warm and dry followed by a rainy period. Cut off the disfigured ears before spores germinate.

Corn earworms and raccoons are major pests. Control earworms with a drop of mineral oil placed on the base of silks as they begin to brown. And the raccoons? Good luck!

History/Folklore

Fossilized grains show that corn has been around for 4,000 years. After the discovery of the New World, corn (called "maize") quickly spread throughout Europe.

Tip

Fresh-picked corn is sweetest because it's high in sugar. If you quickly dunk fresh-picked corn in ice water it will slow the conversion of sugar into starch.

Cucumber

Site

LIGHT: Full sun.

SOIL: Prefers rich soil and abundant organic matter.

Planting

WHEN: Start indoors 6 weeks before last frost, in individual peat pots.

DEPTH OF SEED: 1 inch deep.

DEPTH OF TRANSPLANT: Same depth as in container.

SPACING: 12 inches apart; space rows 48 to 72 inches apart.

DAYS TO MATURITY: 55 to 65 days.

SPECIAL NEEDS: Roots don't like to be disturbed, so transplant carefully. Using individual peat pots minimizes disturbance.

Growing

WATERING: Be consistent. Insufficient watering causes disfigured fruit and reduces flowering. Fluctuating soil moisture also produces a bitter taste in cucumbers.

FERTILIZING: Cucumbers aren't big consumers of fertilizer. Use a formula high in phosphorus and apply at half strength. Be sure to scratch fertilizer into soil around plants as vines begin to flower.

SPECIAL NEEDS: Cultivate the soil often to keep it loose.

Harvest

WHEN: Cucumbers are 6 inches long and dark green in color.

HOW: Twist off vine.

TIP: The longer you leave cucumbers on the vine, the more their quality deteriorates. Fruit production also slows.

Storage

TECHNIQUES: Best fresh or pickled.

STORAGE LIFE: One week in the refrigerator.

Nutrition

Cucumbers are 96 percent water! They also contain a little iron and vitamins.

Pest/Disease Control

Rotate the crop to help reduce problems with cucumber beetles.

History/Folklore

Most likely originated in India. De Soto found cucumbers growing in Florida in 1539.

Tip

Grow cucumbers vertically on a trellis. Keeping them off the ground will save space, keep them clean, and prevent rotting.

Eggplant

Site

LIGHT: Full sun.

SOIL: Likes lots of organic matter so soil will hold water. (Mixing peat into soil works especially well to improve water retention.)

SPECIAL NEEDS: Prefers hot, sunny weather.

Planting

WHEN: Start indoors 6 to 8 weeks before last frost date.

DEPTH OF SEED: $\frac{1}{4}$ inch deep.

DEPTH OF TRANSPLANT: Same as in container.

SPACING: $1\frac{1}{2}$ feet apart; space rows 3 feet apart.

DAYS TO MATURITY: 85 to 90 days.

Growing

WATERING: Consistent, moderate watering is necessary for good fruit production.

FERTILIZING: Apply general garden fertilizer at time of planting, sidedress every 3 weeks until fruits appear, and then once more as fruits are growing.

SPECIAL NEEDS: Eggplant has shallow tea roots so don't cultivate soil around plant.

Harvest

WHEN: Pick once fruit reaches desired size.

HOW: Twist off vine.

TIP: Dull-colored skin is a sign the eggplant is over-ripe. The fruit will be bitter tasting and tough. Egg-plant can be picked at any stage. If fruit becomes overripe its production will be dramatically slowed.

Storage

TECHNIQUES: Store in plastic bag in the refrigerator.

STORAGE LIFE: 5 days.

Nutrition

High in vitamin B_2.

Pest/Disease Control

Hand-pick Colorado potato beetles and tomato horn-worms. Use treated seeds where verticillium wilt is a problem.

History/Folklore

Native to Africa and Asia. The earliest mention is in a fifth-century Chinese book. A black dye was made from eggplants and used by women to stain their teeth to look like shiny metal. In 1806, both white and purple varieties were grown in the United States. The name comes from the old white varieties, whose fruits really look like eggs!

Tip

Has a flavor similar to fried oysters and is often used in dishes as a substitute for meat.

Garlic

Site

LIGHT: Full sun.

SOIL: Likes lots of organic matter, pH 5.5 to 6.8.

SPECIAL NEEDS: Since garlic doesn't like hot weather southern gardeners should plant garlic in the fall for spring harvest. Northern gardeners plant in the spring for fall harvest.

Planting

WHEN: Fall or spring.

DEPTH OF SEED: Garlic is started from individual cloves. Bury 2 inches into the soil, tips up.

DEPTH OF TRANSPLANT: Not applicable.

SPACING: 4 inches apart; space rows 1 foot apart.

DAYS TO MATURITY: 90 days.

Growing

WATERING: Water when dry, but when leaves are a foot high, stop watering.

FERTILIZING: Fertilize in spring when new growth appears—then every 3 to 4 weeks. Fertilizers high in nitrogen are best.

SPECIAL NEEDS: Cutting off water prior to harvest (2 to 3 weeks) prepares garlic for storage.

Harvest

WHEN: Once green tops die down.

HOW: Gently dig up bulbs, leaving the stem intact. Hang in airy location to dry or lay out in the sun to cure, about 1 to 2 weeks.

Storage

TECHNIQUES: Store in a cool, dry, well-ventilated area (not the refrigerator). Do not wash bulb or separate cloves.

STORAGE LIFE: 6 to 7 months.

Nutrition

Vitamin B_1 and minerals.

Pest/Disease Control

Since garlic is an excellent pest repellent, most pests will stay away.

History/Folklore

Believed to ward off evil spirits and disease.

Tip

Dried stems can be used for braiding. Wait until tops have dried on the bulb. Then braid dried greens together, adding more bulbs of garlic as you go. Braiding is great for handling garlic.

Gourd, Edible and Ornamental

Site

LIGHT: Full sun.

SOIL: Prefers light soil. Mix in plenty of rotted manure, compost, or other organic matter. Grows anywhere pumpkins and squash grow.

Planting

WHEN: Sow outdoors after all danger of frost has passed. Areas with a shorter growing season should start seeds indoors.

DEPTH OF SEED: 1 inch deep.

DEPTH OF TRANSPLANT: Not applicable.

SPACING: 18 inches; space rows 3 feet apart.

SPECIAL NEEDS: Gourds grow well on mounds of soil. Plant 5 seeds around the top.

Growing

WATERING: Consistent watering ensures good quality and yields.

FERTILIZING: Too much fertilizer will produce many leaves but not much fruit.

SPECIAL NEEDS: Likes to climb. Give support using a trellis.

Harvest

WHEN: Leave ornamentals on vine until leaves die. Pick edibles as they reach desired size.

HOW: Gently twist off vine. Some may require a sharp knife.

TIP: When the stringy tendril turns dry and brown, the gourd is ripe.

Drying

TECHNIQUES: Wipe but do not wash. Place in warm, dry location. When you hear a rattle inside, the gourd is dry. Small gourds dry in a couple of weeks. Large gourds will take months.

STORAGE LIFE: When dried, they can last a few months to a few years, depending on the variety.

Nutrition

Ornamental gourds should not be eaten.

Pest/Disease Control

Squash bug lays red eggs on undersides of leaves. Scrape off eggs. Damage from the spotted cucumber beetle larvae can be prevented by rotating crops every year.

History/Folklore

Native Americans polished gourds by rubbing them in their hands for long periods of time, coating them with the natural oils in their hands.

Tip

Gourds can be shaped using soft tape or by inserting the young pods in jars. When it is the same size and shape as the jar, carefully break the glass and it will maintain that shape.

Jerusalem Artichoke

Site

LIGHT: Full sun to partial shade.

SOIL: Not picky. Grows well even in poor soil.

SPECIAL NEEDS: This vegetable is perennial, so give it a site where it can stay in the ground for several years. But they are very invasive, so consider planting them in a confined area away from the vegetable garden.

Planting

WHEN: After danger of frost passes and soil warms in spring or fall.

DEPTH OF SEED: Plant tubers 4 inches deep.

DEPTH OF TRANSPLANT: Not applicable.

SPACING: $1\frac{1}{2}$ to 2 feet apart.

DAYS TO MATURITY: 130 days.

SPECIAL NEEDS: Like potatoes, the tuber can be cut into pieces. Just make sure each piece has a number of "eyes."

Growing

WATERING: Plants prefer consistent water, though they'll tolerate some drought.

FERTILIZING: Amend soil before planting.

SPECIAL NEEDS: If you don't harvest enough, they can grow as wildly as weeds. Can grow to be more than 10 feet tall!

Harvest

WHEN: In the fall, when tops die back, usually after first couple of frosts.

HOW: Gently dig up with a fork.

TIP: If ground doesn't freeze hard, you can leave tubers buried for winter harvest.

Storage

TECHNIQUES: Store in a cool location or refrigerate.

STORAGE LIFE: One week.

TIP: Unlike potatoes Jerusalem artichokes don't store well. Their thin skin will shrivel.

Nutrition

Vitamin B, also iron, phosphorus, and potassium. Low in calories, with a sweet nut-like flavor. It stores its carbohydrates in the form of insulin.

TIP: Good low starch substitute.

Pest/Disease Control

They usually are free from pests and diseases.

History/Folklore

French explorers saw Cape Cod Indians growing this relative of the sunflower in 1605.

Tip

Jerusalem artichokes are in the sunflower family. As tubers grow underground, a beautiful spray of yellow daisies appear on top. Eat Jerusalem artichokes as you would a potato or as a crunchy addition to green salads.

Kale

Site

LIGHT: Full sun.

SOIL: Will grow in poor soil but prefers deep, loamy soil. And will tolerate moist soils.

SPECIAL NEEDS: If soil is acidic, mix in lime at least 2 weeks before planting.

Planting

WHEN: Sow seeds outdoors in spring; use transplants for the fall garden.

DEPTH OF SEED: ½ inch deep.

DEPTH OF TRANSPLANT: Same as in container.

SPACING: 2 feet apart; space rows 2 feet apart.

DAYS TO MATURITY: 55 to 70 days.

SPECIAL NEEDS: Flavor of kale comes from rich soils.

Growing

WATERING: Needs consistent watering.

FERTILIZING: Dig in lots of rotted manure or compost before planting. Feed with organic nitrogen every 3 weeks thereafter.

SPECIAL NEEDS: Grows best in cool weather. Well-fed, fast-growing plants taste better.

Harvest

WHEN: Harvest younger leaves. The older they are, the more bitter they become.

HOW: Cut or break off leaves from the base of plant.

TIP: A nip or two from frost will actually sweeten the flavor.

Storage

TECHNIQUES: Kale freezes well. It also stores well on the plant far into winter—you can pick in the snow.

STORAGE LIFE: 5 days in the refrigerator.

Nutrition

Vitamins A, C, and E, iron, calcium, potassium, and phosphorus.

Pest/Disease Control

Use quality seeds to try to avoid flea beetles, aphids, and the Herculean beetle. Mulch also can help.

History/Folklore

Originated in Asia Minor. Vikings brought it to Scotland, where they gave it the name "kale."

Tip

Ornamental varieties of kale are great for fall color in the garden until a hard freeze. As temperatures cool the colors become more vibrant. Kale makes a great garnish. It can be used in a salad like other greens or cooked like spinach. But taste can be marginal.

Kohlrabi

Site

LIGHT: Full sun.

SOIL: Prefers fertile, well-drained soil with pH 6.0 to 7.0. Enrich soil with organic matter.

SPECIAL NEEDS: Add lime if the soil goes below pH 5.5. Mix in a few weeks before planting.

Planting

WHEN: Sow outdoors 3 weeks before last frost and again in late summer for a fall crop.

DEPTH OF SEED: ½ inch deep.

DEPTH OF TRANSPLANT: Same as containers.

SPACING: 6 inches apart; space rows 1½ feet apart.

DAYS TO MATURITY: 45 to 120 days, depending on the variety.

SPECIAL NEEDS: Thinned-out plants can be replanted, but the shock will make them mature more slowly.

Growing

WATERING: Needs consistent watering to prevent splitting; soil should always be moderately moist.

FERTILIZING: After thinning, give them some organic fertilizer and cover soil with mulch.

SPECIAL NEEDS: Grows best in cool days of spring and fall.

Harvest

WHEN: Once bulbs are 2 inches across (some newer varieties grow larger).

HOW: Gently pull and twist or cut with a knife.

TIP: Bulbs are sweeter in the fall after a light frost. The leafy greens are also edible.

Storage

TECHNIQUES: Refrigerate in a plastic bag.

STORAGE LIFE: One week.

Nutrition

Vitamin C, potassium, calcium, and magnesium.

Pest/Disease Control

Suffers from many pests and diseases in the cabbage family. Placing tuna cans without a top or bottom around young plants will prevent cutworm damage. Crop rotation helps prevent club root.

History/Folklore

Originated in northern Europe.

Tip

Should be cooked in its skin to preserve flavor. A fun vegetable for the kids to watch grow.

Leek

Site

LIGHT: Full sun.

SOIL: Prefers loamy soil with abundant organic matter.

SPECIAL NEEDS: Make sure soil has a good supply of phosphorus and nitrogen.

Planting

WHEN: Sow in garden 3 weeks before last frost; start indoors 4 to 5 weeks prior to last frost date.

DEPTH OF SEED: $\frac{1}{4}$ inch deep.

DEPTH OF TRANSPLANT: Same as container. But better if sown directly in garden

SPACING: Thin seedlings to 1 inch apart; space rows 2 feet apart.

DAYS TO MATURITY: 105 to 130 days.

TIP: Larger transplants grow better leeks.

Growing

WATERING: Needs regular watering.

FERTILIZING: Likes heavy applications of well rotted manure. Or sprinkle a 10-10-10 fertilizer around plant 6 weeks after planting.

SPECIAL NEEDS: For whiter stalks, cover base of leek with soil or surround with collar. This technique, called blanching, makes more of the stalk edible.

TIP: Flowers of leeks are edible.

Harvest

WHEN: Late summer when base is 1 to 2 inches in diameter.

HOW: Loosen leek with fork and gently pull.

TIP: Mulch leftover leeks for winter harvest where ground doesn't freeze.

Storage

TECHNIQUES: Refrigerate in a plastic bag or place in a cool, humid location.

STORAGE LIFE: 2 to 3 months.

Nutrition

Vitamin C, calcium, phosphorus, and potassium.

Pest/Disease Control

Onion maggots can be controlled with insecticidal soap or horticulture oils.

History/Folklore

Native to either Algiers or Switzerland. National symbol of Wales and worn by Welsh soldiers in their hats to distinguish themselves from the enemy. Used in sixteenth century as a cure for drunkenness.

Tip

Leeks are less prone to pest problems than onions.

Lettuce

Site

LIGHT: Full sun or partial shade.

SOIL: Loose and crumbly soil. Dig in plenty of manure or compost the previous autumn.

Planting

WHEN: As soon as soil can be worked in spring (same time as you plant peas).

DEPTH OF SEED: Simply press into soil. Seeds need light to germinate.

DEPTH OF TRANSPLANT: None.

SPACING: Space rows 1½ feet apart.

DAYS TO MATURITY: 45 days, although can vary depending on variety.

SPECIAL NEEDS: Grows best in cool weather. Seeds will not germinate when soil temperatures exceed 70°F.

Growing

WATERING: Needs steady supply of water.

FERTILIZING: Nitrogen.

SPECIAL NEEDS: Lettuce will go to seed when temperatures climb into the 90s. Plant small amounts of leaf lettuce every few weeks for a steady supply of tender, sweet lettuce.

Harvest

WHEN: Leaves: Start picking outer leaves when they are about 4 inches long. Leaf varieties will continue to produce until hot weather arrives. Heads: once desired size is reached.

HOW: Cut with shears or sharp knife.

TIP: Picking in the morning will provide crisper leaves.

Storage

TECHNIQUES: Use fresh or refrigerate in a plastic bag.

STORAGE LIFE: 5 days.

Nutrition

Good source of fiber and high in Vitamin A and C. Some iron. Good source of calcium.

Pest/Disease Control

Spread sand over the planting area to prevent rot. Fungal and bacterial diseases can be reduced by annual crop rotation.

History/Folklore

Native to the Mediterranean and Near East. The name derives from the Latin "lac," which means milk and refers to the milky sap that flows from a cut stem.

Tip

What to do with all the leftover lettuce seeds? For the leafy varieties, mix all the seeds together and plant in mid- to late summer. You'll have tossed salad growing right in front of your eyes.

Okra

Site

LIGHT: Full sun.

SOIL: Good drainage is important to prevent seed rot. Likes soil rich in nitrogen with pH between 6 and 7.

SPECIAL NEEDS: Grows best in hot weather.

Planting

WHEN: Sow outdoors after all danger of frost has passed and once soil is 60°F.

DEPTH OF SEED: ½ inch deep.

DEPTH OF TRANSPLANT: Same as in container.

SPACING: 2 to 3 feet apart; space rows 3 feet apart.

DAYS TO MATURITY: 55 to 65 days.

TIP: Soak seed overnight or scratch seed with knife to speed germination.

Growing

WATERING: Keep well watered, especially during dry periods.

FERTILIZING: Add compost or aged manure in the planting holes. Feed with a liquid fertilizer during the growing season every few weeks.

SPECIAL NEEDS: Use collars to protect plant from cutworm damage.

TIP: In warmer climates cut plant back midsummer for a second crop.

Harvest

WHEN: Once pods are about 3 inches long but still soft. (Longer ones can be tough and bitter.)

HOW: Gently snap off pod.

TIP: Pods have spines. Wear gloves when harvesting.

Storage

TECHNIQUES: Refrigerate in a plastic bag.

STORAGE LIFE: 10 days.

Nutrition

Vitamins A and C, calcium, and potassium.

Pest/Disease Control

Hand-picking can control bollworms, stinkbugs, and blister bugs.

History/Folklore

A member of the hibiscus family, originating in Africa.

Tip

Pods left to dry on the plant can be used in dried flower arrangements.

Onion

Site

LIGHT: Full sun.

SOIL: Well-drained, fertile soil high in phosphorus. If soil is acidic add lime a couple of weeks before planting.

SPECIAL NEEDS: Protect from weeds.

Planting

ONIONS ARE PLANTED 3 WAYS: By seed, sets, transplants.

WHEN: In spring as soon as soil can be worked.

DEPTH OF SEED: Small bulbs are planted outdoors ½ inch deep.

SPACING: 4 to 6 inches apart; space rows 12 to 18 inches.

DAYS TO MATURITY: Scallions can be harvested in 35 to 40 days, mature onions in 100 days.

TIP: If planting sets, pick the smallest bulbs when buying.

Growing

WATERING: Be generous and consistent, especially in early growing stage. Dry soil will cause splitting and two smaller bulbs will form.

FERTILIZING: Light application of 10-10-10 every 4 weeks.

TIPS: Weeds will compete for water and nutrients—keep them out.

Harvest

WHEN: Pick when the tops die down and skin around the bulb head turn brownish.

HOW: Pull from soil.

SPECIAL NEEDS: If you're storing onions they must be cured. Let them dry on ground in garden 1 week. Then move to warm, dry location indoors for 2 to 3 weeks. Cut foliage after they're cured and store in mesh bags in cool, dry location.

TIP: As long as they are dry, a light frost will not affect them.

Storage

TECHNIQUES: Store fresh in refrigerator 1 to 2 weeks. Cured onions will keep for another 2 to 3 weeks.

Nutrition

Vitamins B and C, protein, calcium, phosphorus, and iron.

Pest/Disease Control

To help control the root maggot, dig in lots of organic matter before planting.

History/Folklore

Native to western Asia. George Washington was known for his love of the onion. Some farmers believe that thicker-than-usual onion skin foretells a severe winter.

Tip

Don't cut off dried stems—they're great for braiding onions together.

Parsnip

Site

LIGHT: Full sun to partial shade.

SOIL: Rich and well cultivated; grows well in sandy soils. Amend with lots of compost or other organic matter if the soil is full of clay.

Planting

WHEN: Sow outdoors 4 weeks before last expected frost in spring.

DEPTH OF SEED: ¼ inch deep.

SPACING: Thin to 4 to 6 inches apart; space rows 18 inches apart.

DAYS TO MATURITY: 105 days.

SPECIAL NEEDS: Slow to germinate; soak seeds overnight before planting.

Growing

WATERING: Keep soil moist until seedlings emerge, then water as needed.

FERTILIZING: Every 3 to 4 weeks scratch an all-purpose fertilizer into the soil.

SPECIAL NEEDS: For long, straight taproots, soil must be free of large stones or debris.

Harvest

WHEN: In the fall after a couple of light frosts.

HOW: With a spade or garden fork, gently lift roots from soil.

TIP: Can be left underground all winter and harvested when needed. Mulch heavily to delay ground freezing.

Storage

TECHNIQUES: Remove leaves and place in container of moist sand, cover, and keep in cool, dark place.

STORAGE LIFE: Can be refrigerated for a month.

Nutrition

High in Vitamins A and C, also potassium.

Pest/Disease Control

Has very few problems.

History/Folklore

Discovered by Sir Walter Raleigh in South America. Before the discovery of the potato, this member of the carrot family was a staple in European diets.

Tip

Freezing actually improves texture and gives a sweeter taste.

Peas

Site

LIGHT: Full sun to partial shade.

SOIL: Rich, well-cultivated soil.

SPECIAL NEEDS: Prefers cool weather. Use mulch to help keep soil cool.

Planting

WHEN: As early as possible when soil can be worked in spring.

DEPTH OF SEED: 1 to 2 inches deep.

SPACING: 3 to 6 inches apart in two rows 3 to 6 inches apart. Space double rows 2 feet apart.

TIP: Soak seeds overnight to speed germination.

SPECIAL NEEDS: Peas need cool weather to produce. In northern climates, plant in early spring; in southern climates, in the fall.

Growing

WATERING: Be consistent.

FERTILIZING: Add 10-10-10 fertilizer to the soil 2 weeks before planting. Sidedress with more fertilizer every 3 to 4 weeks while growing.

Harvest

WHEN: Peas are young and tender when each pod is just barely plump.

HOW: Gently twist pod from the vine, being careful not to injure the vine.

TIP: Peas on the lower branches will develop earlier.

Storage

TECHNIQUES: Excellent for freezing and drying.

STORAGE LIFE: Use fresh peas immediately because the sugars turn to starch 2 hours after harvest. Can be refrigerated for 1 to 2 weeks.

Nutrition

Vitamins A, B, and C, also protein, magnesium, and iron.

Pest/Disease Control

Rotate the crop to prevent root rot, wilt, and bacterial blight. Can also be attacked by pea aphids and pea weevils. Spray plant with sharp spray of water or dust with rotenone to control.

History/Folklore

Found everywhere in history, including a 9750 B.C. cave dwelling in Thailand and Bronze Age ruins in Switzerland. Peas were a staple and eaten dry until the seventeenth century. Thomas Jefferson declared peas to be his favorite vegetable.

Tip

As peas develop, remember that the more you pick, the more the plant produces.

Peppers, Sweet and Hot

Site

LIGHT: Full sun.

SOIL: Rich in organic matter. Mix in compost or rotted manure before planting.

SPECIAL NEEDS: Grows best in warm weather and warm soil. Black plastic over soil surface helps heat the soil faster.

Planting

WHEN: Start indoors 8 to 10 weeks before last frost date.

DEPTH OF SEED: $\frac{1}{4}$ inch deep.

DEPTH OF TRANSPLANT: Same depth as in container.

SPACING: 18 to 24 inches apart; rows 2 feet apart.

Growing

WATERING: Weekly and during dry periods.

FERTILIZING: Lightly fertilize when planting, using 10-10-10, especially when fruit develops.

SPECIAL NEEDS: When temperatures get hot, mulch plant to help retain moisture and reduce weeds.

Harvest

WHEN: Pick fruit when final color of cultivar is achieved (some will turn green, red brown, yellow, yellow green, depending on which type).

HOW: Remove fruit by cutting stem with a knife or carefully twist with your hand.

TIP: Picking earlier will yield a milder-tasting pepper.

Storage

TECHNIQUES: Good fresh, frozen, and pickled. Can also be dried.

STORAGE LIFE: One week in the refrigerator.

Nutrition

Vitamins A and C; good source of fiber and carotene.

Pest/Disease Control

Place collars around seedlings to prevent cutworm damage. Mosaic produces oddly shaped and colored leaves. Remove and destroy all plants affected with this virus. Rotate every planting season.

History/Folklore

Columbus discovered peppers growing in the West Indies, but mistakenly thought they were a relative of the prized peppercorn.

Tip

If you grow chili peppers, heed your garden center's warnings—hot means hot! Wear gloves when handling hot peppers and remember not to rub your eyes. The pepper's oil can burn on contact.

If you're after a sweeter, more nutritious pepper, redder is better.

Potato

Site

LIGHT: Full sun.

SOIL: Moist, very rich and loamy, acidic soil (pH less than 6).

Planting

WHEN: In cool climates, 2 to 3 weeks before last frost date; in warm climates, late summer or late winter.

DEPTH OF SEED: The "seed" is actually a small potato. Bury 3 to 4 inches deep.

SPACING: 12 inches; space rows 2 feet apart.

DAYS TO MATURITY: 90 to 105 days.

SPECIAL NEEDS: Only purchase certified seed potatoes. Cut seed potato into pieces that contain at least 2 to 3 eyes. (Eyes are the small indentations.) Smaller potatoes are best and don't need cutting. Allow cut pieces to cure or dry for 24 to 48 hours to help prevent the growth of harmful fungi. Traditionally potatoes are grown in trenches about 6 to 8 inches deep. Mix in all-purpose fertilizer before planting. Once planted, cover with 4 inches of soil.

Growing

WATERING: Be consistent, especially during dry periods. Knobby potatoes are a result of inconsistent watering. Cavities will also develop inside potatoes from inconsistent H_2O.

FERTILIZING: Fertilize with nitrogen in July, when the plants begin to blossom.

SPECIAL NEEDS: When the potato grows to 4 inches tall, mound soil up and around the stems, leaving only the top showing. Keep mounding the soil around plants until first flowers appear.

Harvest

WHEN: Carefully dig for new potatoes when blossoms appear. For large potatoes, wait to dig until plants begin to turn brown.

HOW: With a garden fork or your hands, dig down in dry soil and lift carefully.

Storage

TECHNIQUES: Don't wash potatoes if you plan on storing them. Keep in a cold and dark location.

STORAGE LIFE: 4 to 9 months if potatoes are cured. Fresh potatoes—1 week in refrigerator

Nutrition

Vitamins B_1, B_2, and C, also iron, potassium, calcium, and phosphorus. The leaves and stems are poisonous.

Pest/Disease Control

Watch for Colorado potato beetles, flea beetles, leafhoppers, aphids, and wireworms. Potatoes are susceptible to disease called "scab." It's not fatal but not appealing. It looks like small, rough scabs on the skin of the potato. Alkaline soils encourage scab. "Late Blight" is also a problem.

History/Folklore

Native to Peru. In the sixteenth century, Spanish explorers introduced it to Europe. The Irish were the first Europeans to use the potato as a staple. In 1845, late blight struck the Irish crops and caused widespread famine, which led to mass emigration to the New World.

Tip

Do not plant in same spot where potatoes, tomatoes, or other related vegetables grew in previous two years. Dig in rotted manure the fall prior to planting.

Pumpkin

Site

LIGHT: Full sun.

SOIL: Prefers sandy loam.

SPECIAL NEEDS: Prefers a location that doesn't get much wind.

Planting

WHEN: Sow outdoors after all danger of frost. Or start seeds indoors a few weeks before last frost.

DEPTH OF SEED: ½ to 1 inch deep.

DEPTH OF TRANSPLANT: Same as container.

SPACING: Give them plenty of room to roam. Each plant will spread 10 feet or more!

DAYS TO MATURITY: 105 days.

SPECIAL NEEDS: To grow larger pumpkins, remove all female flowers as soon as one or two fruits begin to form. This conserves energy to help the existing fruits grow larger.

Growing

WATERING: Water weekly or if soil is dry.

FERTILIZING: Fertilize every 3 to 4 weeks.

TIP: To ensure ripe pumpkins in the fall, remove new blossoms after 4 to 5 fruits have formed.

Harvest

WHEN: Once skin turns hard and achieves proper color for cultivar–deep orange.

HOW: Cut 3 to 4 inches of stem with a knife.

TIP: Seeds make a great, nutritious snack when roasted in an oven. Just wash seeds, pat dry, sprinkle with salt. Bake at 350 to 400°F until seeds turn golden brown. Stir once while baking.

Storage

TECHNIQUES: Pumpkins and jack-o'-lanterns will rot if they freeze. Store in warm, dry location with temperatures between 50 and 60°F.

STORAGE LIFE: 2 to 3 months.

Nutrition

Seeds are rich in protein; pulp is rich in vitamin A.

Pest/Disease Control

Plant rotation will help prevent diseases.

History/Folklore

Mexican Indians grew their seeds more than 7,000 years ago. The tradition of carving a jack-o'-lantern originated in Ireland and Scotland, when potatoes and turnips were decorated with hideous faces to ward off evil spirits.

Tip

Once you've carved the pumpkin, coat the cut edges with petroleum jelly to keep it from shriveling.

Radish

Site

LIGHT: Sun to partial shade, with at least 6 hours of sun per day.

SOIL: Sandy loam rich in nutrients, but not too much nitrogen.

SPECIAL NEEDS: Radishes get hot tasting and woody if temperatures are too warm.

Planting

WHEN: In spring as soon as soil is workable for northern gardens and again in fall. For southern gardens, plant in fall for a winter crop.

DEPTH OF SEED: ½ inch deep.

SPACING: 1 to 2 inches; space rows 6 inches apart.

SPECIAL NEEDS: Sow seeds every 1 to 2 weeks for a continuous harvest.

TIP: Radishes grow very quickly, making a great plant for kids to grow.

Growing

WATERING: Keep soil moist for best quality and milder flavor.

FERTILIZING: None needed unless you have sandy soil, then a light application of 10-10-10 needed once.

SPECIAL NEEDS: Grow quickly and harvest promptly for best flavor.

Harvest

WHEN: As soon as radishes reach desired size.

HOW: Gently pull foliage tops.

TIP: Radishes that sit in the ground become woody and strong flavored.

Storage

TECHNIQUES: Remove tops and refrigerate in a plastic bag.

STORAGE LIFE: 3 weeks.

Nutrition

Vitamin C and some minerals.

Pest/Disease Control

Not many pests, but watch for root maggots. To help control maggots, avoid growing radishes in an area where a member of the cabbage family grew in the past 3 years.

History/Folklore

Most likely from the Mediterranean. Prized by the ancient Greeks and eaten by the Egyptians. Used to cure kidney stones by British herbalists. Comes from the Latin word "radix," meaning "root."

Tip

Since they are quick growers, radishes are often sown among other crops to mark the planting rows.

Rhubarb

Site

LIGHT: Full sun or light shade.

SOIL: Since rhubarb is a perennial, it's important to amend the soil well and deeply (18 inches) prior to planting. Well-drained, loamy soil with pH 5.5 to 6.5 is ideal. Enrich with well-rotted manure or other organic matter before planting.

SPECIAL NEEDS: Permanent plant. So select location carefully. Grows best during cool, moist summers. Grows best in northern half of the country (zones 3 to 7).

Planting

WHEN: Plant roots in early spring when soil is workable.

DEPTH OF TRANSPLANT: Use 2- to 3-year-old roots, and set 4 inches deep or so the buds are 2 inches below the surface.

SPACING: 3 feet apart; space rows 4 feet apart.

TIP: Make sure each plant has two buds or "eyes."

Growing

WATERING: Plenty.

FERTILIZING: Enrich soil before planting. Rhubarb is a heavy feeder. During the second year you should scratch in 10-10-10 fertilizer in the early and late spring and again in the fall.

SPECIAL NEEDS: During the first year it is necessary for plant to establish a good root system. Let it grow but no harvesting.

TIP: Rhubarb will send up two kinds of stalks. The edible stalk is a leaf stalk. The other kind is a round flowering stalk. Cut these down before they flower. Otherwise you won't get as many leaf stalks.

Harvest

WHEN: None the first year. The second year, harvest only 1-inch stalks late in July. The third year, enjoy!

HOW: Cut stalks at base with knife or quickly twist stalk at base.

TIP: Don't harvest all the stalk at once. Leave at least ⅓ to ½ to keep plant healthy and strong. Early harvests tend to have a better flavor. Don't harvest in late summer unless you're going to move plants at the end of the season.

Storage

TECHNIQUES: Refrigerate stalks in a plastic bag.

STORAGE LIFE: 2 to 3 days.

 Nutrition

Vitamin C. Don't eat the leaf blades because they are poisonous.

Pest/Disease Control

Leaf-eating pests can be picked off by hand. Foot rot can affect the base of stems, causing them to turn mushy and rot. Dig out entire plant and dispose of by burning. Don't plant rhubarb in the same spot.

History/Folklore

Originated in Siberia. Grows wild in Asia (Turkey, India, and China). Rhubarb was cultivated by American gardeners in the eighteenth century.

Tip

Dig up and move after 6 to 8 years of growth. As the plants get older, the stalks get thinner and smaller.

Spinach

Site

LIGHT: Full sun or partial shade.

SOIL: Rich and well-drained.

SPECIAL NEEDS: Soil should be tilled to a depth of 6 inches.

Planting

WHEN: As soon as soil can be worked in spring or late summer for fall crop.

DEPTH OF SEED: $\frac{1}{2}$ inch deep.

SPACING: 1 inch apart; space rows 12 inches apart.

TIP: Stop sowing seed late May; early June weather gets too warm for spinach.

Growing

WATERING: During dry spells, the area should be soaked late in the day.

FERTILIZING: Use fertilizer high in nitrogen such as fish emulsion.

SPECIAL NEEDS: Thin plants to about 8 inches apart. (Eat the thinnings!)

Harvest

WHEN: Any time after leaves are about 3 to 5 inches long.

HOW: Pick outer leaves. The center ones will continue to grow.

TIP: Clean leaves and dry quickly. Moisture left on leaves will break down or dissolve vitamins and affect flavor. Also cook quickly to retain vitamins and minerals.

Storage

TECHNIQUES: Refrigerate in a plastic bag.

STORAGE LIFE: 3 days.

Nutrition

Vitamins A and C, folic acid, and iron.

Pest/Disease Control

Not many problems. Most insects can be protected with floating row covers.

History/Folklore

Spinach originated in Persia. It spread to China by 647 A.D. and to Spain by 1100 A.D. Colonists spread it to the New World.

Tip

Spinach is most nutritious when eaten raw. Heat will affect the fresh taste of spinach, so harvest before it gets too hot.

Squash, Summer

Site

LIGHT: Full sun.
SOIL: Well-drained, fertile soil with pH 6.0 to 6.5.

Planting

WHEN: Sow outdoors after all danger of frost has passed.
DEPTH OF SEED: 1 inch deep.
DEPTH OF TRANSPLANT: Same as in container.
SPACING: 3 feet; space rows 5 to 8 feet depending on variety.
DAYS TO MATURITY: 50 to 60 days.
SPECIAL NEEDS: Planting squash on mounds of soil is beneficial. Encourages good drainage and soil warms quickly. Start with 6 seeds to a hill. Thin to 2 plants.

Growing

WATERING: Be generous.
FERTILIZING: Enrich soil with a fertilizer high in phosphorus (5-10-5) prior to planting.
TIP: The first yellow flowers, without any fruit at the base, are male flowers. They can be eaten. Clean and stuff with cheese and herbs. Bake to warm inside.

Harvest

WHEN: Pick when small, 6 to 8 inches long; skin should be able to be penetrated with fingernail.
HOW: Carefully cut squash from the vine with a knife.
TIP: Harvest daily to keep fruit production going.

Storage

TECHNIQUES: Refrigerate. Freezes well.
STORAGE LIFE: 1 to 2 weeks.

Nutrition

Vitamins A and C.

Pest/Disease Control

Powdery mildew, fusarium wilt, and mosaic virus can cause problems. Young plants can fall prey to cucumber beetles and squash bugs. Cover plants with lightweight landscape fabric (floating row cover) to protect. Remove as soon as flowers appear to allow pollination.

History/Folklore

Squash is native to America and was a staple for the Native Americans. Dried squash were used as containers.

Tip

If your garden lacks space, plant squash among corn.

Squash, Winter

Site

LIGHT: Full sun.

SOIL: Well-drained and fertile, with pH 6.0 to 6.5.

SPECIAL NEEDS: Needs room to roam. Smaller varieties can be staked or trellised to keep fruit off the ground.

Planting

WHEN: Start seeds indoors 4 to 6 weeks before the last frost. In warmer climates sow outdoors after all danger of frost has passed.

DEPTH OF SEED: 1 inch deep.

DEPTH OF TRANSPLANT: Same as in container.

SPACING: 4 feet apart; space rows 6 feet apart.

DAYS TO MATURITY: 85 to 120 days.

SPECIAL NEEDS: Winter squash take twice as long to mature as summer squash.

Growing

WATERING: Be generous.

FERTILIZING: Mix 5-10-5 fertilizer into soil prior to planting.

SPECIAL NEEDS: Mulch soil, as fruits on the ground can rot quickly.

Harvest

WHEN: Once fruits are completely mature and vines begin to turn brown, or two weeks before first frost.

HOW: Cut 1 to 2 inches of the stem with sharp knife.

Storage

TECHNIQUES: Must cure in sun or warm room for 1 to 3 weeks before storing. This toughens the outer skin.

STORAGE LIFE: Varies with variety.

Nutrition

Winter squash is more nutritious than summer squash. Vitamins A and C.

Pest/Disease Control

Squash vine borers should be cut out of the vine; cover the cut vine with soil to encourage it to re-root.

Tip

Pumpkins are considered a winter squash.

Tomato

Site

LIGHT: Full sun.

SOIL: Loose, fertile soil with pH 6.0 to 7.0. Enrich with organic matter prior to planting.

SPECIAL NEEDS: Allow 3 years to pass before planting in the same space to reduce pest and disease problems.

Planting

WHEN: Start indoors 10 weeks before last frost. Move outdoors after last frost.

DEPTH OF SEED: ¼ inch deep.

DEPTH OF TRANSPLANT: Same as in container.

SPACING: 18 to 36 inches apart; space rows 3 feet apart.

DAYS TO MATURITY: 54 to 90 days. Most varieties take 60 to 80 days.

SPECIAL NEEDS: When I plant tomatoes I dig two holes: one for the tomato plant, the other for a small handful of 10-10-10 fertilizer.

Growing

WATERING: Must be very consistent. Widely fluctuating watering can promote blossom-end rot or cracking.

FERTILIZING: Mix in 10-10-10 fertilizer prior to planting, then lightly scratch in 5-10-5 fertilizer every 4 to 5 weeks.

TIP: Tomatoes drop flowers and won't grow fruit if temperatures drop below 50°F or rise above 90°F.

SPECIAL NEEDS: Some people remove the suckers or shoots that develop in the crotches of the branches. This is not necessary but will help maintain a stronger plant and will concentrate energy in the main branches.

Harvest

WHEN: As tomatoes are turning from pink to red.

HOW: Gently twist from vine.

TIP: For best flavor, allow to ripen on the vine.

Storage

TECHNIQUES: Can be frozen, canned, and dried. Do not refrigerate.

STORAGE LIFE: Fresh, about a week. Use frozen within 6 to 9 months. Dried and canned tomatoes are good for years.

Nutrition

Vitamins A and C, potassium, and iron.

Pest/Disease Control

Control cutworms with collars. Aphids can be controlled with ladybugs, lacewings, or insecticidal soaps. Hand pick tomato hornworms. Resistant tomato varieties will control verticillium, fusarium wilt, and nematodes (look for VFN) on plant markers.

History/Folklore

Native to Peru, although the tomato grew wild all over South America, Central America, and Mexico. Brought to North America in the sixteenth century. Reputed to be an aphrodisiac.

Tip

Don't refrigerate, as the cold reduces the flavor quickly. If you must pick green tomatoes (as before a hard frost), allow them to ripen in a dark location that is approximately 60° to 70°F.

Turnip and Rutabaga

Site

LIGHT: Full sun best but will tolerate partial shade.

SOIL: Loose, well drained, and fertile, with a pH of 6 to 7.

SPECIAL NEEDS: Rotate site at least every 2 years.

Planting

WHEN: When soil can be worked.

DEPTH OF SEED: $\frac{1}{4}$ inch deep in cool weather; $\frac{1}{2}$ inch deep in warmer weather. Space rows 2 feet apart.

DEPTH OF TRANSPLANT: Same as in container.

SPACING: Thin seedlings to 4 inches apart; space rows 18 inches apart.

DAYS TO MATURITY: 35 to 70 days.

SPECIAL NEEDS: Germinating seeds can't push through hard crusty soil. Be sure site is tilled or aerated prior to planting.

Growing

WATERING: Once a week or when soil is dry. Turnips and rutabagas will split if watering is inconsistent. Be consistent.

FERTILIZING: If you amended your soil don't fertilize. Otherwise scratch in a 10-10-10 fertilizer every 3 to 4 weeks.

TIP: Harvest young greens 4 weeks after planting.

Harvest

WHEN: Once they reach 2 to 3 inches in diameter (the size of a tennis ball). When they get larger they become bitter tasting. Harvest before temperatures get hot.

HOW: Gently pull from soil.

TIP: A couple of frosty nights will improve flavor.

Storage

TECHNIQUES: Refrigerate in a plastic bag or put in a cool, humid environment.

STORAGE LIFE: 4 to 5 months; greens 10 to 14 days.

Nutrition

GREENS: Vitamin A, calcium, potassium, and iron.

Pest/Disease Control

Choosing disease-resistant varieties will prevent many problems.

History/Folklore

Grown in China since 200 B.C.

Tip

To extend harvest, heavily mulch plants.

Zucchini

Site

LIGHT: **Full sun.**
SOIL: **Rich and well drained.**

Planting

WHEN: **After all danger of frost is past.**
DEPTH OF SEED: **½ to 1 inch deep.**
DEPTH OF TRANSPLANT: **Same as deep container.**
SPACING: **1 foot apart; space rows 5 feet.**
DAYS TO MATURITY: **50 to 55 days.**

Growing

WATERING: **Once a week at the base of the plants.**
FERTILIZING: **Every 3 to 4 weeks.**
SPECIAL NEEDS: **Keep weeded.**

Harvest

WHEN: **As soon as zucchinis reach 4 to 8 inches long.**
HOW: **Twist from vine.**
TIP: **Check plant every few days since fruits grow quickly.**

Storage

TECHNIQUES: **Refrigerate in a plastic bag.**
STORAGE LIFE: **1 week.**

Nutrition

Vitamins A and C.

Pest/Disease Control

Rotate the crop annually to reduce the numbers of striped cucumber beetle.

History/Folklore

Not widely known in the United States until the 1950s.

Tip

Zucchini are prone to blossom-end rot.

Index

Spurge (*Euphorbia*), 23
  cushion, 25
Squash
  summer, 174
  winter, 175
Stakes, natural, 27
Staking, 33–34
  stretch-tie, *33*, 33–34
Statice (sea lavender), 25
Stepping stones, making your own,
    133–34
Stinkweed, 124
Stone paths
  laying your own, 134
  plants for, list of, 132
Sunflower seeds, roasted, 64
Sunflowers, 19, 63, 88
  fort, 20
  harvesting, 64
  planting, 63–64
  wreaths, *104*, 104–105
Sunscald, 97
Sweet alyssum, 18, 120, 132
Sweet gum, 95
Switch grass, 68

Thyme
  creeping, 132
  woolly, 132
Tickseed (*Coreopsis*), 25
Tomatoes, 8, 120, 176
  blight, 58–59
  dried, 82
  fried green, 82–83
  ripening green, 81–82

storing, 8
  Wall-O'-Waters and, 8–10, *9*
Tools
  choosing, xiii–xiv
  cleaning, 103–104
  neon, 136–37
Topiaries, 127–29, *128*, *129*
Toxic plants, list of, 123–24
Trees, 29
  balled-and-burlapped, 30, 31
  bare-root, 30–31
  basic needs of, 29–30
  buying, 30–31
  common problems in, 34–35
  in containers, 30, 31
  fall care of, 95–97
  for fall color, list of, 95
  flowering, 36–37
  mowing around, 66
  planting, 31–33, *32*
  pruning, 34
  staking, 33–34
  watering and feeding, 34
  winterizing, 97
  see also Christmas trees; individual
    names
Trillium, 25
Trough gardens, 138–39
Trowels, xiv
Tubers, 92
Turnips, 177

Vegetable gardens
  fall care of, 81–85
  fertilizing, 6, 58